The 20 British Prime Ministers
of the 20th century

Blair

MICK TEMPLE

HAUS PUBLISHING · LONDON

First published in Great Britain in 2006 by
Haus Publishing Limited
26 Cadogan Court
Draycott Avenue
London SW3 3BX

www.hauspublishing.co.uk

Copyright © Mick Temple, 2006

The moral right of the author has been asserted

A CIP catalogue record for this book is available from the British Library

ISBN 1-904950-73-6

Designed by BrillDesign
Typeset in Garamond 3 by MacGuru Ltd
info@macguru.org.uk

Printed and bound by Graphicom, Vicenza

Front cover: John Holder

Contents

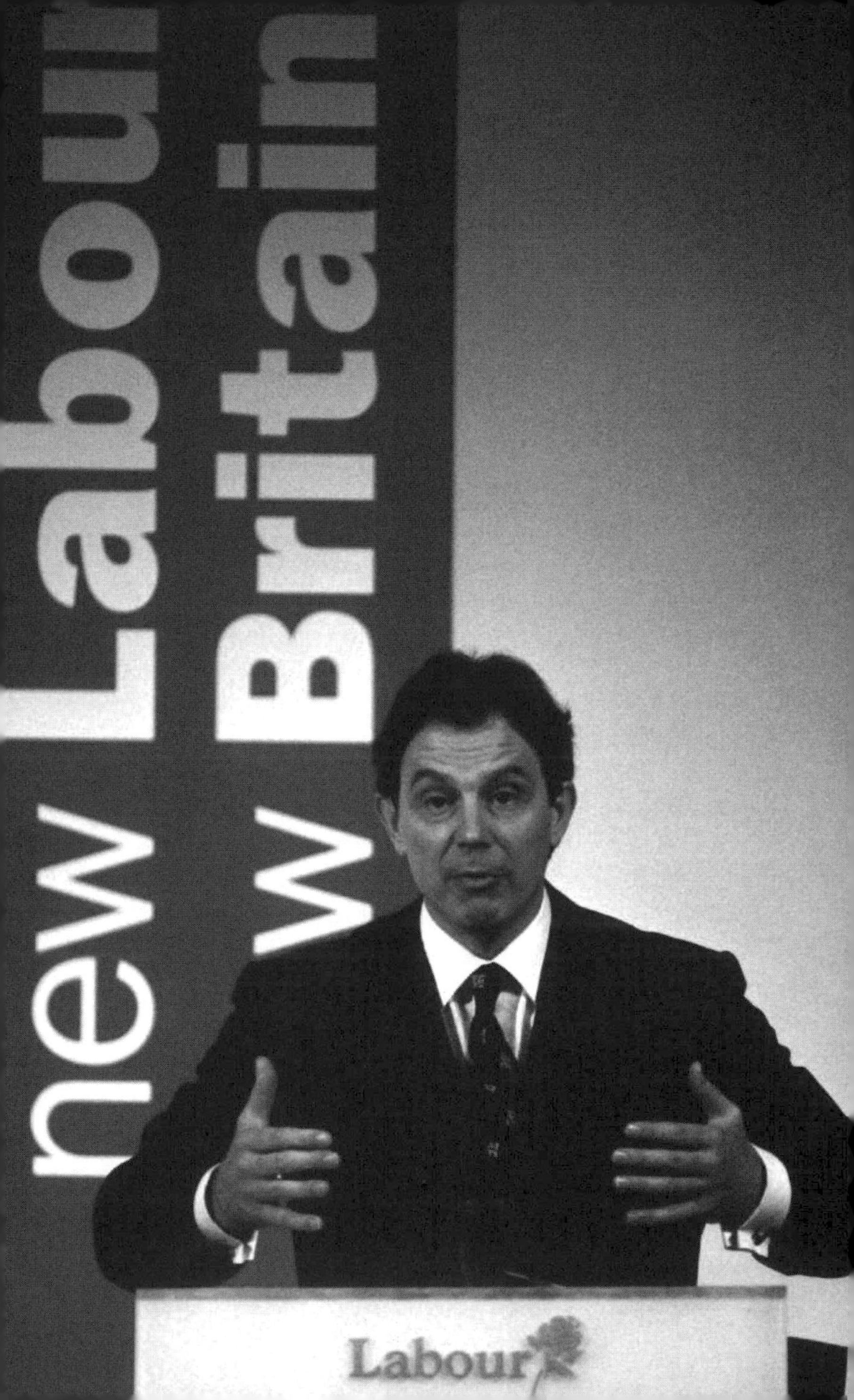
new Labour
new Britain
Labour

Introduction

No British politician has entered prime ministerial office riding the wave of goodwill and public optimism upon which Tony Blair swept into Downing Street. In 1997, an ineffective and decidedly uncharismatic Conservative government had limped along until the last possible moment before calling an election. John Major's Cabinet had lost the party its reputation for economic competence; his Chancellor could jokingly remark, 'je ne regrette rien', after losing more than £10 billion of our money. 'Sleaze' dominated the political agenda. Cash in brown envelopes for asking parliamentary questions, marital infidelity and kinky sex with everyone and everything from rent boys to schoolgirls, inappropriate directorships and shady dealings all smacked of pigs at the trough. Overall, the Conservative government gave an impression of being out of touch with popular feeling and decidedly 'yesterday's men'.

A government of largely old and grey men seemed out of place, survivors of an ancient regime, in the new 'Cool Britannia' of the 1990s, where British groups like the Stone Roses, Blur and Oasis were once again setting new pathways for popular music and hot young British fashion designers were evoking memories of the Swinging Sixties. Thatcherism and its central tenet of market ideology as the solution for all problems no longer captured the mood of what appeared to be a more caring and consensual political environment.

The nation wanted something younger, fresher and cleaner, and Tony Blair and New Labour appeared to encapsulate all the needs of a 'New Britain'. Britain was a country that did not want to return to the strife-ridden pre-Thatcherite days of the 1970s, with states of national emergency, three-day weeks and endless strikes. We wanted a more caring and supportive environment for those at the bottom of society than 'care in the community' but without a return to the nanny state and over-powerful trade unions. Tony Blair promised to deliver it.

This brief biography of Blair cannot claim to be authoritative – but neither can any of his biographies. They are either tainted by too close co-operation with their subject, generally hostile to Blair or essentially speculative. The high degree of secrecy (for a public figure) which Blair has successfully erected around both his private life and the decision-making process at the centre of government also makes accurate assessment difficult for the moment. Assessing the relevance of any living person is fraught with difficulty, especially when that person is a political leader still in office. When Margaret Thatcher left office in 1990 the critical consensus was that many of her major reforms were essentially minor or would soon be reversed. It took a decade for the weight and permanence of her achievements to be realised and even now both respect and the laws of libel restrain her biographers.

His lifelong friend and colleague Anji Hunter doubts that any book can do justice to Tony; 'no one can evaluate him properly' she has declared, and for the moment she is probably right.[1] Any definitive biography of a public figure has to wait until he or she is dead. History may come to a very different judgement on Tony Blair than this slim volume. Whether or not history will regard him as a great man, he is clearly a very important figure in Britain's political history. My purpose here is to outline some of the key events of this public yet very private man's life and attempt a critical appraisal of his achievements. Hopefully, readers will be interested enough to read more in-depth accounts of the life and politics of Anthony Charles Lynton Blair.

Part One

THE LIFE

Chapter 1: Tony Blair's Childhood

All his biographers have commented upon Tony Blair's desire for secrecy in both his public and private life. Elements of his family background may be an important contributory factor in this concern. At first glance, Tony Blair appears to have been born into an ordinary middle-class family, one perhaps relatively privileged by the standards of the time, but apparently representing certain solid values of family and religion. His father Leo Blair, a former army officer, had trained as a lawyer and when Tony was born had a post as a law lecturer at Edinburgh University. Leo's Conservative Party membership further supports the picture of an almost stereotypically conventional middle-class family, albeit one where the father had ambitions to become an MP. Behind this normality, the reality is more exotic.

Tony Blair bears a remarkable physical resemblance to his mother. His emotional closeness to her was considerable; she was the rock of his early life and her strong religious conviction was passed on to him. Perhaps crucially for her son's development, she did not wholly share her husband Leo's centre-right views. Hazel Blair is the key to Tony Blair's core beliefs. She was born Hazel Corscaden in 1923 in Ballyshannon, County Donegal, Ireland, into a devout Protestant family. Her father died when she was just six months old and her mother married a Ballyshannon man, William McLay.

The family moved to Glasgow where Hazel's stepfather became a successful butcher. From what little we know, her home life was happy and stable. She left school at 14; despite possessing a quick intelligence (as well as an occasionally hot temper) her education was limited, not unusual for women then. When war broke out she joined the Navy as a Wren, visiting Australia in the course of duty. The war over, she went to work as a typist at the Ministry of National Insurance in Glasgow where she was eventually to meet Tony's father.

Leo Blair was born in 1923, the illegitimate son of two touring variety actors. His mother, Celia Ridgeway, was already married, although she was later divorced by her husband for her adultery and married Leo's father Charles Parsons in 1926. Charles' stage name was Jimmy Lynton; Leo was later to adopt Charles and Lynton as his own middle names and his two sons were to be christened William James Lynton and Anthony Charles Lynton. Celia and Charles asked Mary and James Blair, who had become friends during shows in Glasgow, if they could look after baby Leo until they were able to give him a greater degree of stability. Information is sketchy about his natural parents' subsequent contact with their son, although when they later tried to remove the 13-year-old Leo from his foster parents, Mary threatened to commit suicide if he left.[1] Leo stayed, and assumed for many years that his natural parents had subsequently lost interest in his life.[2] As Anthony Seldon has noted, it is impossible to gauge the precise effect of such emotional turmoil upon Leo, but a sense of abandonment and rejection was to affect him all his life. In fact, they had written many times to him but Mary had first hidden and later burned the cards and letters. She eventually wrote to Celia and Charles telling them he was missing, killed in action, and his parents died never knowing the truth.[3]

Such a cruel act by an essentially kind and decent woman, who adored Leo and was adored by him in turn, can only be explained by his status in her life. After two miscarriages she had been unable to bear children and Leo was an unexpected blessing. Her husband James, a shipyard rigger (when work was available in the harsh realities of the 1930s Depression) was frequently ill and died young. Leo was the centre of her life and to lose him would have been more than she could bear. She gave him everything, encouraging and supporting him in his wish to better himself. He showed his debt to his foster parents a few months before his marriage to Hazel, when he changed his name by deed poll from Parsons to Blair.

While he was given great love and support, Leo's upbringing was harsh. Tenement living in Govan bred toughness and left-wing politics were the norm. His foster mother was a staunch Communist and Leo imbibed the language of Marxist-Leninist ideology. He went to work for the party newspaper the *Daily Worker* when he left school. He was an active Communist Party member and, intelligent and blessed with considerable organisational ability, he began to think seriously about a career in politics. His wartime experiences, as with many other servicemen, were to radically change his politics, but Leo went in the opposite direction ideologically to most of his compatriots. He began the war as a private but in the 'people's war' class barriers were being broken down. He was commissioned and found to his surprise that he enjoyed the company of the officers' mess. His foster mother had instilled in him a desire for self-improvement and his discovery that men on the other side of the class war were far from the demons he had been told they were weakened his faith in Communism and convinced him that Conservative ideology made a lot of sense. He had no desire to spend his life in a tenement block sharing an outside toilet with other families. Although he voted Labour in 1945, by 1947 he had joined the Conservative Party.

Intelligent and motivated, upon discharge from the army as a second lieutenant he began studying part-time for a law degree at Edinburgh University while working full-time for the Inland Revenue. He met Hazel and they fell in love. Upon qualification he began working at the university as a law lecturer, a considerable indication of his intellectual abilities; he must have made a very favourable impression upon his own tutors. He taught himself to play the piano, singing popular songs well to his own accompaniment, and friends and acquaintances found him charming and amusing company. In 1948 he married Hazel and their wedding picture shows an attractive and personable looking couple. For Jon Sopel, Leo Blair was a 'walking advertisement for social mobility'.[4]

Despite some biographers' assertions of a strong, often authoritarian father, Tony speaks of him with clear affection, while acknowledging that for the first 11 years of Tony's life his father's political and business interests made him a relatively remote figure. What veteran Labour parliamentarian Leo Abse described as a 'house of secrets' may be at the core of Blair's personality. Abse's entertaining (if highly speculative) psychological examination of Blair supports the sense of both father and son as outsiders. Abse alleges that the spectre of Celia, whom he calls judgementally Tony Blair's 'promiscuous grandmother', hung over Leo Blair and the family. Amazingly, Blair told his early biographer Jon Sopel that he was unaware of the origins of his Christian names and had been surprised when Sopel informed him.[5] As Tony Blair has remarked, his father's parentage was something that was not a topic of conversation. Abse argues the reason neither he nor his brother asked was because they knew it was a question they must never ask; 'secret, forbidden territory'.[6]

Arguably, secrecy, even down to his essential beliefs, has been a characteristic of Blair's life. As one of his schoolteachers was later to note, 'you couldn't call him reserved, but you never saw his real self. He didn't like to expose himself in case someone spotted a weakness [and] he has always been conscious of how he appears to other people.'[7] It is entirely possible that this sense of secrecy relates back to the shame Leo Blair felt about his parentage. In the days before the sexual revolution of the 1960s, illegitimacy brought with it real social stigma.

'He [Blair] *didn't like to expose himself in case someone spotted a weakness* [and] *he has always been conscious of how he appears to other people.'*

DAVID REYNOLDS

William Blair was born in Edinburgh in 1950, and Anthony Charles Lynton Blair followed three years later on 6 May 1953. The coronation less than a month later of the young Queen may have been heralded with cries of a new Elizabethan age but Britain in the 1950s was a grey, conformist world where compulsory national service still existed and memories of wartime dominated. The certainties of Empire and British superiority had yet to be questioned. In late 1954, the Blair family sailed for Australia, where Leo had obtained a post as a lecturer in administrative law at the University of Adelaide. Leo and Hazel's third child, Sarah, was born in Australia in 1956, completing the family. Although they were there for just three years, some maintain you can still hear a tinge of Antipodean in Blair's vowels.

The family enjoyed their time in Adelaide, living in a pleasant house in the eastern suburb of Dulwich. Both Leo and Hazel had known real hardship in their childhood and the welcoming atmosphere of Australia was refreshing after the constraints of British society. Blair told Anthony Seldon that Australia – with its can-do attitude, laid-back approach to social niceties and relative lack of class-consciousness – affected him deeply and its people and culture were to be a 'profound influence' on him throughout his life. Given that he was four when he left and can have few if any memories of his time there, it's difficult to see how the country could have had such a lasting influence. However, coming from the openness and brightness of Australia to a cold, dark British winter cannot have been too pleasant for any of the family.

Returning to Britain in early 1958, the family settled in the university city of Durham. When they left Britain, post-war austerity had still bitten hard, but the country was now experiencing the fruits of an economic boom. Leo lectured at the university but his ambitions for himself and his children required a more affluent lifestyle and practising law, rather than merely teaching it, would provide this. Leo was called to the Bar and set up his own law practice in Newcastle upon Tyne. The practice prospered and his ambitions to become a Conservative MP were reignited. He became Chairman of Durham's Conservative Association and his hopes of a winnable parliamentary seat were nearing fulfilment. The family moved from the centre of Durham, close to the university, into a new four-bedroom house on the edge of the city. They were a two-car family in an age when one car was a luxury. Most years, they holidayed in Ireland, close to Hazel's birthplace. The family was upwardly-mobile, popular with their neighbours, and seemed to be an exemplar of Harold Macmillan's boast that Britons 'had never had it so good'. Clearly, Leo Blair was a man to watch; charming, talented, hard-working and politically ambitious. There appeared no limit to his prospects.

Bill was entered into the renowned Durham Chorister

School, while Tony went to Western Hill, a private 'pre-pre-paratory school' for the children of the affluent middle classes. Three years later he joined his elder brother as a dayboy. Both boys were very happy at Choristers; Tony, as the younger of two brothers at the same school, was known as 'Blair Two'. Neither brother was a chorister, but otherwise both took a full part in school life. Tony played rugby and cricket for the school teams, was a keen athlete, acted in a number of school productions (although only in minor parts) and was a leading participant in school debates. According to his headmaster he was the sort of boy who was 'the backbone' of the school.[8] He was popular with both his fellow pupils and with the staff. A recurring theme throughout Tony's life and a consid-erable part of his early political appeal is his ability to charm women. The school matron, Rita Jakes, quickly became an 'ally and confidante'[9] and her support at school was to be invaluable during the first major crisis of his young life.

In July 1964 the family's life was changed forever and Leo's political ambitions permanently ended. In the early hours of 4 July, American Independence Day, Leo had a severe stroke. He was 40. Tony was woken early next morning by his mother and knew immediately that something serious had happened. Despite the tragedy, Tony was sent to his normal Saturday morning school session and, that afternoon, Hazel came from the hospital to watch him play rugby for the school. She told him his father was 'probably going to live'.[10] Leo had come very close to death and his recovery was slow. For the next three years he struggled to regain his speech, helped patiently by Hazel. His university salary continued and he gradually returned to teaching duties, but his law income was severely cut. Their social position suffered and one of the cars had to be sold. More importantly, shortly afterwards young Sarah was in hospital for two years with a form of childhood rheumatoid arthritis. Hazel's devotion and commitment to her family was crucial, and guided Tony through what must have been a traumatic experience. Although Leo was often away on both legal and party business (he was a popular guest speaker with Conservative Associations) and may have been a more distant figure than many modern fathers, his influence on the family was considerable and Tony Blair's fondness and respect for his father remains apparent.

Outwardly, Tony continued to present the same smiling and likeable persona to his schoolmates and teachers. Undoubtedly, the closeness and warmth of his family – Bill returned for the summer holidays from Fettes College and his solid good sense was invaluable – combined with the pastoral care of the staff at Choristers, helped him. Hazel's stepfather's contribution to the boys' school fees was also important in maintaining family spirits; the fall in the family's income would not be allowed to affect Bill and Tony's schooling and dent their future chances of success.

Tony's apparent lack of emotional response to his father's illness has been hinted at by biographers as something unnatural, but children, especially those with the support of a strong and loving family, are generally tougher than they are given credit for. It's also probable that the sense of privacy which has seemed to his biographers a feature of both Tony Blair's public and private life, perhaps instilled by Leo's anxieties about his own illegitimate background, was important. Keeping it in the family meant that Tony kept such emotions for his mother's eyes. He later admitted that he became emotionally aware for the first time that *nothing is permanent*; it was *the day my childhood ended.*[11] But whatever the shock of his father's sudden illness, Tony Blair clearly regards his early childhood in Durham and his time at Choristers School as happy. This childhood happiness was to be challenged by his move away from home to boarding school.

In 1966, Tony entered Fettes College in Edinburgh, 'Scotland's Eton' as it liked to be known. A rather forbidding set of buildings and a new set of arcane rituals would have been daunting to any boy, but unlike many new boys Tony's prep school experiences had been as a dayboy at a school where pastoral care was an important ingredient. His mother's daily affection had been crucial in the difficult years following Leo's stroke. He was relatively unprepared for dormitories, dodgy institutional food and pupil-administered discipline. Tony also had a lot to live up to at Fettes. His brother Bill had already been there for three years and was enormously popular and academically successful, eventually gaining a prestigious scholarship to Balliol College, Oxford. Tony was put into Bill's house and as he had won a scholarship in the school's entrance examinations he went straight into the second year, studying with boys mostly one year older than him.

There is some disagreement among his biographers about his experiences during his first year at Fettes. For example, Seldon argues that in his first year, 'all went well' whereas Beckett and Hencke maintain that he 'had a miserable first year'.[12] Whatever the reality, all agree that after the first few terms he was unhappy there and became a school rebel, albeit one who was careful not to cross the line that would have meant expulsion. Blair and his close friends loved the Lindsay Anderson movie *If ...,* released in 1968, which detailed violent rebellion at an English public school where all the worst Victorian excesses of caning and fagging were still carried out. Fettes still clung to such traditions and more, including the rigorous enforcement of what appeared to be pointless distinctions in clothing and privileges. Fags were effectively 'slaves' to senior pupils, and their duties ranged from making toast (which Tony was apparently very good at) to making up fires. Senior boys could cane junior boys almost on a whim, often excessively, and Tony was caned on a number of occasions. It must have been an awful time. The world outside was changing, swinging England was calling, and there he was locked in an archaic and, to him, barbaric environment, away from the warmth of his home. Gradually, and as many public schoolboys elsewhere were also doing, Tony grew to resent the pettiness of many of the rules, although his rebellion stopped short of machine-gunning staff, pupils and parents as in Anderson's acclaimed satire.

Undoubtedly, his rebellion would have been fuelled by a serious academic embarrassment in his first year. Working with older boys, he struggled to keep up and was demoted to the first year group. Although his progress after this initial setback was academically satisfactory, he must have felt some humiliation at this slight. Whatever the reasons, his school career after his first year was marked by shows of dissent and frequent, if generally petty, clashes with authority. Famously, aged 14, he tried to run away on his return to Fettes for his second year. Delivered by his parents to the Edinburgh train, he walked through the carriages and off the train, left Newcastle station and made his way to Newcastle airport. In those less security-conscious times he apparently made it onto a plane bound for who knows where but was discovered by a stewardess. His parents made sure he stayed on the train the next time.

Realising that he was stuck with the school, it appears he decided to make the best of it, while still bucking the system as far as possible. Blair's rebellion was on the edges. For example, by his third year, despite his undoubted prowess at the main school sports of rugby and cricket where he would certainly have made the senior second teams and had a chance of progression to the starry heights of the First XI or First XV, he preferred to captain the basketball team and play association football. Such decisions by a potentially good performer in the 'establishment' sports would not have endeared him to most masters.

However, there was one school tradition he enthusiastically embraced. The actor in Tony Blair was apparent from early on. Acting had a rich tradition at Fettes and for his house production of *Julius Caesar*, Tony was given the key role of Mark Anthony over the claims of more senior boys. He was to play key roles in future school productions, including Captain Stanhope in R C Sheriff's *Journey's End* and Drinkwater in George Bernard Shaw's *Captain Brassbound's Conversion*.[13] His dramatic acting and his performances in revues were widely praised and more than one of his compatriots or tutors is convinced he could have had a successful career as an actor. Not to be flippant, there are some who would argue that he did; an essential part of his early political appeal was to be able to convince whoever he was talking to that they shared deep political beliefs.

Despite his success at sport and acting, Tony Blair had had enough of Fettes by his final year, and it is clear Fettes had had enough of Tony Blair. Despite his 'general bolshiness' he might have expected to become at the very least a house prefect but instead was beaten in this final year for 'persistent defiance'. John Rentoul reports that the teachers he spoke to all said they were glad to see the back of 'a complete pain in the backside'.[14] Eric Anderson, Blair's housemaster and an inspiring English teacher, has frequently been cited as an early mentor. The reality is more complex. Anderson was responsible for the decision to deny Tony the opportu-

> *'A complete pain in the backside.'*
>
> FETTES STAFF ON BLAIR

nity to become a prefect and thought he took advantage of the trust shown in him; behind Anderson's back, Tony was openly contemptuous of him. Anderson described Blair as one of the 'most challenging boys' he had ever met.[15] Much to Anderson's embarrassment, they were re-united at Number 10 in late 1997 for a series of teachers' recruitment advertisements where celebrities such as the England goalkeeper David Seaman nominated a teacher who had influenced their life. Blair nominated Anderson, who after Fettes became headmaster and then Provost of Eton, as his favourite teacher. Coincidentally, Eric Anderson also taught Conservative leader David Cameron when he was at Eton. Seldon maintains that Anderson's influence on the young Blair was modest.[16]

The dreariness of day-to-day existence was partially relieved by forbidden pub-crawls of Edinburgh, a dangerous activity as expulsion could have resulted. He constantly sang and played guitar, although he does not appear to have been especially proficient at either singing or playing. But his love of rock music and his idolisation of Mick Jagger and the Rolling Stones gave him a role model and he grew his hair as long as possible within the school rules. He specialised in petty disobedience, and often turned up for classes late or wearing the 'wrong tie'. He

Blair's former Fettes housemaster, Robert Roberts, saw his former pupil on television and at once sat down and wrote a poem which ended:

'You smile and talk away out there
Just as you did when you had me
To check your facts and trim your wings;
But now you're free and on the air,
I've no more opportunity
To expose your specious arguings.'

(*Worm's Eye View* by Robert Roberts, Pikestaff Press, Devon, 1995.)

was once driven by Eric Anderson to the barber's shop and given a short back and sides, a humiliation that makes his later citing of Anderson as a mentor seem somewhat bizarre. Eventually, the catalogue appears to have grown so much that he was threatened with expulsion. Although two boys in Blair's year had been expelled for drug-taking, and the soft-drug culture at Fettes was well known, Tony's offences were probably nowhere near as serious. Once again, the obsession with secrecy that characterises Blair's life is demonstrated when trying to find out more about his final months at Fettes. In the conformist world of the British public school, it is probable that his tutors had just had enough of this irritating young man.

Following the intervention of teachers and perhaps of a family friend who was an old Fettesian, Blair was allowed to take his 'A' levels, although he was also caned, an unusual punishment for a member of the upper sixth. He left school immediately after his exams and was 'pushed off to university as fast as possible'.[17] His grades have been carefully guarded by the school at his request, another sign of how he defends the tiniest details of his life. However, it appears that he took three 'A' levels, gaining very respectable grades; an A in English, an A in History and a C in French.[18] Balliol, his brother Bill's college, turned Tony down, but he won a place at St John's, also in Oxford. He asked to defer his admission in order to take a gap year. For many students, gap years were for touring the world or working for voluntary organisations overseas. Tony had one aim – to make it in the rock music business, preferably as a performer, and there was only one place in Britain to head for. London was calling to the faraway towns.

He left Fettes without regrets. In the next few years, Tony Blair was to experience a number of key events that were to shape his life. His developing religious faith was to be cemented by meeting at Oxford a man who, unlike Eric Anderson, really did impact on his life, Peter Thomson. Most importantly, the early death of his mother, who gave him the belief in his own abilities and who his biographers agree was the major influence on his worldview and political philosophy, was to change him forever.

Chapter 2: Oxford, the Bar and Cherie

At Fettes, where most boys conformed, Blair had been something of an icon of cool. Such status was to be subject to sterner examination in the hedonistic world in which he now moved. In late summer of 1971, he arrived in London carrying only a small suitcase and a cheap home-made guitar, which he rather pretentiously named 'Clarence' in the style of great blues players like B B King. After a few weeks of bumming accommodation from friends of friends he struck lucky when he met Alan Collenette, another personable ex-public schoolboy. The two quickly became good friends and Blair stayed with Alan at his parent's home in Kensington for the rest of the year.

Still strumming his guitar and dreaming of stardom, he was quickly disillusioned. He really wasn't good enough and, unlike at Fettes, a more sophisticated audience greeted his efforts with disdain. Collenette had a better idea. Promoting rock bands required no musical talent and promised big cash returns. 'Blair-Collenette Promotions' was born, after some arguments about the order of their names, which Tony won of course. They eventually secured the church hall of the Vineyard Congregational Church in Richmond as a regular base. The legendary Blair charm was again evident and he soon moved into a room in the house of the retired schoolmaster who supervised the use of the hall and ran a Christian youth club there. Tony and Alan named the venue the Vineyard and began promoting their first gig, handing out flyers outside local schools. Blair, with his winning smile, good looks and unchallenging sexuality was extremely attractive to young girls and Alan Collenette remembers that their first question to Tony was often, 'will you be there'?[1]

A relatively competent band of ex-public schoolboys, Jaded, were their first act. They regarded Blair with some suspicion and no little amusement, while he was apparently in some awe of their musical proficiency. Tony Blair was an unlikely rock manager or promoter. In the drug-orientated and sexually promiscuous world of 1970s progressive rock, he appeared ultra-straight. Band members and acquaintances remember him as a pleasant and friendly guy, but also as someone who 'never got drunk, never smoked marijuana, never abused women ... and would sooner die than tell a dirty joke'.[2] While in no way promiscuous, especially by the standards of the time, his peers are sure Blair gained in sexual experience during his time in the rock business.[3]

The business itself was decidedly low key. After six months of fairly successful small church hall gigs, during which Blair occasionally sang, they tried to put on a much bigger night at the Queen Alexandra Hall. The bands booked were unknowns, and far too insignificant to fill such a big hall. Only a handful of punters turned up and the gig was a financial disaster; it signalled the end of his fledgling career as a rock impresario. He had made little money from promoting, and occasional department store work supplemented by money from home had been necessary for survival. But it had been an extremely pleasant interlude where he had matured rapidly and made some good friends. He was 18 years old. After a few weeks in Paris, the calmer waters of academia were waiting.

In early October 1972, Tony Blair entered St John's College,

Oxford. He'd wanted to read history but it was much easier to get a place reading law, and three years later he took his law finals and graduated with a decent second-class degree. His time at Oxford is surprising, not for what happened but for what didn't happen. Here was a man who was to become the most charismatic politician of his generation, Labour's most successful leader ever in terms of winning elections, and yet he left little trace of himself. As Seldon notes he was 'almost invisible'; he is not remembered as a debater, politician, actor or sportsman, despite his considerable skills in these areas. Contemporaries such as Peter Mandelson and Benazir Bhutto, a future Prime Minister of Pakistan, were significant presences in Oxford student life. Mandelson does not remember Blair at Oxford and attributes this to the fact that, unlike Blair, he was interested in politics.[4] While there is some evidence of a nascent political animal during Blair's undergraduate years – he flirted around the edges of left-wing groups and once delivered a paper on Marxism – he was totally uninterested in student politics. He attended only one Union debate, to hear Michael Heseltine, then seen as a future Conservative Party leader. What is especially puzzling is that, although he performed in some revues and acted in *The Threepenny Opera* at Oxford Playhouse during his first year, his acting career fizzled out.

His time at Oxford is now largely remembered for his membership of a rock band, Ugly Rumours, who put on no more than a handful of gigs to fellow students. Despite his lack of success as a big-time rock promoter, Tony had not given up hope of pop stardom. A bunch of musicians who needed a lead singer had spotted his stagecraft during a college revue and asked him whether he fancied joining the band – and of course he did! With his long hair flowing, wearing purple loons and a shirt undone to the navel, 'finger wagging and punching the air',[5] his one brief moment of minor notoriety at Oxford was for his Mick Jagger impersonation. He sang well enough, if derivatively, yet he was clearly ill at ease in the rock milieu. His growing Christianity conflicted with the norms of rock and yet again, his musical colleagues remember him as 'straight' – perhaps the most serious insult one could level in the world of 1970s 'head' music.

Contemporaries remember him as passionate about music and as far more interested in religious ideas than political ones. Peter Thomson, an Australian priest and mature student at St John's, had a serious impact on Blair's beliefs. He introduced Blair to the writings of the Christian philosopher John Macmurray, whose ideas on community helped Blair make sense of his thoughts and were to re-appear in the jumble of ideas that informed New Labour philosophy. Thomson was an exciting and charismatic figure who encouraged Blair to think seriously about God and grow more confident in the relevance of his religion to contemporary social problems. Before Peter Thomson, his Christianity had been typically English, something that one vaguely believed in but which had little relevance in day-to-day life. Blair's religion then was intensely private and he never sought to convert others to his faith. At the age of 20 he was confirmed into the Church of England, but even his close friends were largely unaware of this, one of the most significant moments in his life. Thomson's contribution to Tony's intellectual and spiritual development cannot be overstated and he has become a close family friend. The Blairs have holidayed at Thomson's farm in Victoria and the two men still communicate regularly.[6]

For his first two years he lived in college and for his final year he shared a house with one male and three female students, who remember the time (and the man) fondly. He had plenty of girlfriends, played some college football, and enjoyed a good social life of parties and informal gatherings. He kept his hair long, dressed in a 'hippie' fashion, smoked occasionally, drank moderately and eschewed drugs. He also, especially during his final year, worked hard enough to get a decent degree. He was an able yet unexceptional student and no one could have predicted anything other than a prosperous, middle-of-the-road legal career as his most reasonable expectation. At Oxford he had also renewed his acquaintance with Anji Hunter, a friend from Edinburgh parties. Their relationship was extremely close, which was later to cause concern in one half of the Blair household. She had lost her own mother at an early age and was a source of considerable comfort when the most shocking event in Tony Blair's young life interrupted his post-graduation idyll.

Two weeks after Tony's graduation, Hazel Blair died in hospital, aged 52. She had suffered from throat cancer for four years but in the final months her condition had rapidly deteriorated. Her declining state had been kept from her younger son in order not to affect his Finals. Tony Blair has admitted that life took on an urgency previously lacking; his mother's untimely death made him realise that life was too short to continue wasting it on unimportant matters. John Rentoul's belief that Tony Blair's ambition began with his father's stroke does not ring true.[7] There is little evidence that the young Tony's political career was ignited as Leo's ambitions were lost although it does constitute a useful biographical device. Neither his schoolmates and teachers at Fettes, nor his acquaintances at Oxford, remember a man who seemed destined for a political career. His dalliances with politics at university appeared essentially superficial and peripheral to his main concerns. In contrast, his friends and family noted a new seriousness of purpose about him when his mother died. As Seldon memorably puts it, he realised that time was not infinite and a 'steel entered his soul'.[8] He adored her and the central rock of his life was gone. Leo was devastated by Hazel's death and the tragedy brought Tony and his father closer together than they had ever been.

Within a year of his mother's death he was to meet another strong woman and fall in love with her. Cherie Booth is the single most important person in Tony Blair's life and her influence on him is incalculable. The support of his new-found religious faith had been vital in helping him cope with the loss of his mother. It was almost inevitable that his life partner would be someone with a similarly strong faith, and her Catholicism is something he has increasingly adopted, but Cherie's influence has gone far beyond the spiritual. She was to help shape his political beliefs and provide powerful support for his burgeoning political ambitions.

She was born in 1954 in Bury, Lancashire, the eldest daughter of aspiring actors Gale Smith and Tony Booth. Her father later found fame as the 'Scouse git' son-in-law of the racist, working class ultra-Conservative Alf Garnett, in the ground-breaking 1960s BBC comedy *Till Death Do Us Part*, but her childhood was far from the middle-class stability of the Blairs. Her alcoholic father had a number of affairs, some resulting in children (she has six half-sisters), and he finally left home when Cherie was nine and her sister Lyndsey was seven. Life was hard but with the strength and support of her mother she prospered. Unlike her future husband, she was successfully raised a school year and got four 'A' levels, all at the highest grade. She joined the Labour Party at 16 and although unequivocally left-wing she was strongly opposed to the far-left Militant Tendency then taking over Liverpool Labour Party. She won a scholarship to study law at the London School of Economics (LSE) and was active in student politics, especially against the Militant Tendency. Academically she was excellent; clever and hard working, she was awarded one of the best first-class law degrees in the LSE's history.

She won another scholarship for the one-year course to prepare for the Bar exams which all prospective barristers must pass. She came top in the country. Her lecturers recommended her to a leading Queen's Counsel, Derry Irvine, and he agreed to take her as his only pupil. She was disappointed to discover that he later agreed to take on another pupil, Tony Blair, whom she had already briefly met; unlike Cherie, Tony had only a third-class pass in his Bar exam. At the end of the year, she knew only one of them would be taken on as Irvine's tenant, and with the well-known emphasis the profession places on being a 'good chap' she must have already feared the worst. Despite Derry Irvine's acknowledgement that she was a better lawyer, at the end of that year he chose Tony. Irvine was to be a huge help to Tony's advancement, nurturing his legal skills and providing him with important political contacts in the Labour Party. Tony was more affable and much more at ease with a wide range of people while Cherie was seen as brilliant but 'brittle' – she lacked the qualities that were to make her future husband such a successful politician. However, such a potentially brilliant barrister soon found a position at another chambers.

Tony had never met anyone like Cherie – she was passionate, intelligent and wonderful company. While not conventionally beautiful she was striking. In her boyish and slightly dishevelled appearance in a photograph taken of the two of them in Tony's chambers in 1980, she bears an uncanny resemblance to modern-day pop star Pete Doherty. Blair offered something missing from her life, a man she could trust. All who know them, friend or foe, agree on one thing – they adore each other and are ideally matched. Whatever the normal ups and downs of any relationship, and they are certainly uninhibited about arguing with each other in front of friends, there is no doubt their life together has been very happy. Seldon disputes John Rentoul's view of Cherie as having a pivotal role in decision-making, saying she cared more about him gaining power than what he did with it,[9] and New Labour's policies in government certainly don't chime with what we know of her early beliefs. But Blair's governments have been full of left-wingers, from Blunkett to Boateng, who appear to have made Damascene conversions. After 30 years together, she remains the most important overall influence on Tony Blair and it is likely he listens to her opinion before making major decisions.

Tony and Cherie got engaged in 1977 while on holiday in Italy; three years later they married in the chapel of his old college, St John's, where Tony had also been confirmed. Leo Blair had suffered another stroke and Tony Booth had been seriously injured after setting his flat on fire while drunk, so both were absent; Derry Irvine gave the bride away. Her father's injuries effected reconciliation with his daughter, and he gave up drink for good. Even sober and reformed, his ebullient and opinionated father-in-law continued to possess the capacity to unsettle Tony Blair. However, although Booth has criticised the treatment of the elderly, as a life-long socialist he has been remarkably reticent in comments about a government whose policies he must generally abhor.[10]

Chapter 3: Tony Blair, Fledgling Politician

Shortly after meeting Cherie, Tony also joined the Labour Party. Both of them had political ambitions, and to those in the know Cherie's appeared more likely to be fulfilled. Her commitment to the party was undoubted and her brand of soft left socialism was clearly informed by her life experience. Blair, his beliefs less well-formed and often unclear, was regarded with scepticism and suspicion by some party members. Within the Labour Party, Tony Blair has never quite fitted in. Unlike Cherie, his attachment to the party appears superficial and he has never seemed at ease with its rituals and traditions. One can easily believe that, given different circumstances – falling in love with a woman who was a lifelong Conservative, perhaps – Blair would have become an equally charismatic and flexible Tory leader assuming control in the chaos that followed John Major's departure. But both of them fervently opposed the star of the hard left, Tony Benn, and were attracted by Neil Kinnock's energy and charm. Despite this, Tony Blair was also making friends on the centre-right of the party such as Roy Hattersley.

Cherie and Tony had a deal; whoever got into Parliament first, the other would financially support them. After a few failures, in 1982 Tony obtained the Labour nomination for an unwinnable seat in a by-election at Beaconsfield. Cherie's father Tony Booth turned up with his actress partner Pat

Phoenix (Elsie Tanner of *Coronation Street*) to support Blair but despite such celebrity endorsement Labour's percentage of the vote fell dramatically and he lost his deposit. However, he had been noticed. Key Labour figures were impressed but with the 1983 election fast approaching he had yet to obtain a nomination for another seat and he had no intention of standing for Beaconsfield again. Cherie was standing in Thanet North, a safe Tory seat. There was no chance of winning but she was highly regarded by the party and if she did well a safe Labour seat would almost certainly follow. With less than six weeks to go to the election, Tony had still not found a seat. Then, the extraordinary good luck that has characterised key moments in Blair's political career came to his rescue. If he had failed to get into Parliament in 1983 he would have been too inexperienced to be considered a serious leadership candidate in 1994 when John Smith died. Gordon Brown would probably have become Labour leader. Blair's ability to make influential connections probably helped him gain a winnable seat.

The former mining community of Sedgefield in Durham was a new constituency formed after boundary changes. Margaret Thatcher's snap election call caught the local party on the hop. With less than a month to the election they had a safe seat to offer and no candidate. The story of that selection process is enshrined in the Blair mythology and repeated by local agent John Burton in his account of their relationship and relatively uncritically by many chroniclers of Blair's progress. One branch, Trimdon, had yet to nominate a candidate for the selection process. Blair turned up at Burton's home, they hit it off and Blair was added late to the list of candidates as Trimdon's nomination. Burton, captivated by Blair's very real charm, worked hard to persuade local activists that Blair, despite his 'posh' accent and public school background, was the right man for Sedgefield.

Francis Beckett and David Hencke, in their entertaining and polemical appraisal of Blair's life, present a powerful and well-documented case that Blair's selection was effectively a trade union fix at Hattersley and Kinnock's behest. By the time of the selection meeting, Blair had received another nomination from the powerful Transport and General Workers Union (TGWU). Allegedly, a number of unconstitutional decisions were taken throughout the selection process. Burton, a county councillor and seasoned political animal, must have known there were powerful forces behind Blair but his version is radically different: helped by Burton's endorsement, Blair's enthusiasm, youth and energy captivated the local party.[1] The final ballot vote was 73–46 in Blair's favour.

Constituency activists believe that New Labour began in 1983 in Trimdon when John Burton fell for Tony Blair and the future Prime Minister found a man who could provide bedrock support for his belief in modernisation. In Burton's words, 'life would never be the same again for any of us'.[2] John Burton became a key political intimate, one of the few people whose judgement Blair trusts on 'common sense' issues. Burton shared Blair's view that Labour needed reforming in order to become a party of mass appeal rather than vested interest. He also shared the Blairs' deep religious conviction and Burton's loyalty to Tony Blair has been 100 per cent. Aged 30, Tony Blair was duly elected for Sedgefield and entered the House of Commons as Labour's youngest MP.

'Life would never be the same again for any of us.'

JOHN BURTON

The Labour Party in the late 1970s was riven by internal conflict; although the labels are unclear and overlapping, factions from the left, centre and right of the party fought for control. Labour was at war with itself. An unpopular

Conservative government led by Margaret Thatcher watched thankfully as Labour effectively ensured its own unelectability. In 1981, four key senior figures, including Roy Jenkins (later to become one of Blair's political mentors and confidants) left to form the Social Democratic Party (SDP). Initial opinion polls suggested the SDP could win the next election. Labour was led by Michael Foot, a well-loved and essentially decent man who belonged to an earlier political age when perhaps substance counted for more than style. Dishevelled, duffel-coated, nearly 70 but looking even older, and with the air of everybody's favourite dotty granddad, Foot was a disaster in the television-dominated hustings of modern electoral politics. A divided party went into the June 1983 election on a manifesto which advocated withdrawal from Europe and unilateral nuclear disarmament, facing not only a triumphant Falklands War leader who had allegedly 'put the great back into Britain' but also a new and popular centre alliance. Labour's manifesto was famously described by Labour MP Gerald Kaufman as 'the longest suicide note in history'. A landslide Conservative victory and comparative success for the SDP/Liberal Alliance (who despite coming third polled almost as many votes nationwide as Labour) raised doubts that Labour would ever govern again.

Cherie's political career was effectively over. Tony's MP's salary was dwarfed by her earnings at the Bar and he soon gave up law to concentrate on politics. Their first child Euan, conceived during the election campaign, was born in January 1984. Nicholas followed in 1985 and Kathryn in 1988. They were a modern couple, Tony helping with the children he plainly adored whenever possible. But Cherie was the breadwinner, paying for the nanny essential to a career couple and the gradual up-market house moves. She kept her maiden name professionally, taking silk in 1995 and becoming

Cherie Booth, Queen's Counsel. She is highly successful in her own right, a potential High Court judge, and the couple have always regarded themselves as equal partners. If she feels resentment at giving up her own potentially glittering political career (and many doubt that her more acerbic personality would have been helpful to political success) she has never shown it.

Tony Blair's first major act as an MP was to attach himself to the person he clearly expected to become the new Labour leader, Neil Kinnock. Tabloid taunts of 'Welsh windbag' and two general election defeats in 1987 and 1992 (the latter arguably snatched from the jaws of victory by his premature triumphalism) have tainted Kinnock's memory; history may be kinder and judge him on his contribution to making Labour electable. In those early years of his leadership, until too much attention to the marketing men and their focus groups blunted his appeal, Kinnock offered an exciting alternative to Thatcherism. Blair was hooked. Kinnock was duly elected Labour leader with Roy Hattersley as his deputy.

> **Neil Kinnock** (b. 1942) first entered Parliament in 1970 as MP for Bedwellty. Elected to Labour's NEC in 1978, he was appointed to the Shadow Cabinet as education spokesman following Labour's defeat in the 1979 general election. He became party leader in 1983, and was responsible for defeating the Militant Tendency at the 1985 party conference. Kinnock began the modernisation of the Labour Party, but lost the 1992 election and resigned. He was a European Commissioner from 1995 to 2004, and accepted a peerage in 2005.

Very early on as an MP, Blair made connections with people who were to be key players in his future. Gordon Brown became a friend and Blair also impressed Alastair Campbell, then a journalist close to both Neil Kinnock and his wife

Glenys. Blair's old friend Anji Hunter joined him to work in his political office and he met Philip Gould, the party's polling and election expert. Crucially, Kinnock ensured that in 1985 Peter Mandelson became the party's Director of Campaigns and Communications, although most of the mechanisms that were to establish 'Mandy's' reputation as the prince of spin were already in place. These five people – Brown, Campbell, Hunter, Gould, and Mandelson – were to be Tony Blair's core 'political soulmates' as his career prospered.[3]

An early appearance on BBC's *Question Time* went well and Blair continued his drive towards making the party more appealing to 'ordinary' people with articles on how Labour needed to become the 'people's party' again, an early example of Blairspeak. He cultivated the powerful and made a favourable impression with the party leadership. Mandelson was quick to spot Blair's potential. His position gave him huge power, and he used it to promote Gordon Brown and Tony Blair in the media.

Chapter 4: The Road to the Leadership

The 1987 election delivered a comfortable win for Tony Blair in Sedgefield and another landslide victory for the Conservatives. The result was not unexpected by the Labour leadership who, realistically, were aiming to win at the next election.

In 1987 Blair stood for election to the Shadow Cabinet and came close to winning a place. Although not in the Shadow Cabinet, he was promoted to City and Consumer Affairs spokesperson as number two to Bryan Gould (then seen as a future prime minister) on the Trade and Industry team. But Gordon Brown was the coming star, temporarily taking over from John Smith as Shadow Chancellor when Smith suffered a heart attack. However, Blair made an excellent start. He was generally impressive at the despatch box and had a notable success when weighing in against the amoral actions of the City following the stock market crash of October 1987. In 1988 he joined the Shadow Cabinet as Shadow Secretary of State for Energy and in 1989 he was promoted to the key post of Shadow Employment Secretary.

If Labour was ever to have any chance of being in government again, the need to 'modernise' was becoming apparent. For the modernisers, Labour's traditional links with the trade unions and its commitment to public ownership of the 'means of production' (enshrined in the party's Clause IV) were barriers to electoral support. The Thatcher government's privatisation of public companies had been generally popular with the key voters Labour needed to target. Only limited progress towards reform would be made before the 1992 election but Blair's contribution was critical. Despite his debt to the TGWU regarding his Sedgefield nomination, he had a low opinion of trade unions and their leaders. Very early on, Blair recognised the unions would have to be marginalised if Labour was to appeal to key swing voters in the post-Thatcherite environment. His biggest moment came when he announced that the party was abandoning its support for the union closed shop, whereby in some key industries employees had no option but to belong to a particular trade union. While the announcement angered the trade unions it sent a powerful 'moderate' message to the electorate. It also marked out Blair as a coming man.

On the same day as Blair's historic announcement, Peter Mandelson was selected as Labour candidate for the safe seat of Hartlepool. His position as Director of Communications was clearly incompatible with the need to campaign in Hartlepool during a general election. Kinnock, who had perhaps become over-reliant on Mandelson, failed to establish a relationship with Mandelson's successor, John Underwood, who soon resigned. Long-term stalwart David Hill took over as Director of Communications; Hill was to perform a similar service for Blair following Alastair Campbell's departure.

Elsewhere, Kinnock was ensuring that the electorate would at last see the Labour Party as a potential government. The far left, characterised by Arthur Scargill of the National Union of Mineworkers and Derek Hatton who effectively led Liverpool City Council, and a host of left-wing councils that a largely Thatcherite print media termed the 'Loony Left', were seen by the leadership as Labour's biggest electoral liability. Despite Hatton's expulsion from the party in 1986 for membership of Militant Tendency, Labour was still seen by the electorate as a haven for such 'extremists'. Margaret Thatcher had enemies made in heaven – whatever reservations undecided voters might have had about her, the fear of extremist rule by proxy was enough to deter many from voting for Labour. The head of Number 10's Policy Unit under Blair's premiership, David Miliband, was later to point out that New Labour lacked 'dragons to slay', maintaining that Margaret Thatcher had been defined by her enemies (for example, Galtieri and Scargill) as much as by her policies.[1]

Kinnock took on the Militants, promoted a 'soft centre left' policy agenda, and started the process of politically neutering the unions that both John Smith and Tony Blair were to continue. However, despite policy changes and an attempt to rebrand the party the electorate remained unconvinced. Labour's long association with the trade unions was too strong for it to be easily severed – or forgotten by suspicious voters.

Arthur Scargill (b. 1938) was elected President of the National Union of Mineworkers in 1981, having led the Yorkshire miners in the 1974 strike that brought down the Conservative government of Edward Heath. Conflict with the Thatcher government was seen as inevitable, and the miners' strike of 1984–5 was one of the bitterest industrial conflicts of the 20th century. It ended in defeat for the NUM, and the political power of the trade unions was effectively broken. Scargill founded the Socialist Labour Party in 1996 in opposition to New Labour from the left, but it has had little electoral impact.

Margaret Thatcher's increasing personal unpopularity with some key sections of the electorate had been hinted at by an excellent European Parliament election for Labour in 1989 when they won 45 seats and were the largest single party.

Thatcher's uncaring image was seen as a positive for Labour. However, her commitment to introducing the so-called 'Poll Tax' to replace the local rates generated mass protest and a frightened party ditched her. Even some supporters felt she'd been in office too long and her removal was a blow for Labour's election chances. Her replacement, John Major, got rid of the Poll Tax. A campaign to present Major's dull image as a positive advantage – 'honest John' on his soap-box – was bolstered by Operation Desert Storm's successful liberation of Kuwait after its invasion by Iraq. In the run-up to the election, Blair was not optimistic, privately telling a number of people he expected Labour to lose, although the polls suggested otherwise. Labour's opinion poll lead fell away rapidly during the final week but, even so, both the ITV and BBC exit polls predicted a hung parliament. However, the Conservatives won with an overall majority of 21 seats, leaving the psephologists with egg on their faces.

When John Major (b. 1943) was suddenly promoted from Chief Secretary to the Treasury to Foreign Secretary by Margaret Thatcher in 1989, a survey by *The Economist* magazine found that only 2 per cent of respondents had ever heard of him. Yet on 28 November 1990 he succeeded her as Prime Minister. Although his premiership saw progress in Northern Ireland, he was plagued by opposition to his European policy within his own party, and his government never recovered from the economic disaster of 'Black Wednesday' in 1992. (See *Major* by Robert Taylor, in this series.)

Why did Labour lose in 1992? The loss of Mandelson may have contributed to an incoherent and ill-organised campaign and many blamed Shadow Chancellor John Smith's tax plans, successfully attacked by the Tories as 'Labour's Tax Bombshell'. But for the veteran pollster Bob Worcester (of MORI fame) the deciding factor was undoubtedly Labour's disastrous election rally in Sheffield a week before the election. The TV spectacular, with its light show, confetti and singing of the Red Flag was an exercise in 'gaudy triumphalism'. Kinnock's performance, with his roars of 'all right!' to the applause on his entrance, seems to have aroused all the reservations middle Britain had about him and Labour. The defeated Kinnock swiftly resigned as party leader. The result reactivated the fundamental question of whether Labour could ever win a general election. A flood of academic papers and broadsheet newspaper columns answered the question in the negative.

Neither Gordon Brown nor Tony Blair had much chance of winning the leadership in 1992. Both lacked experience, and although Brown could have stood in order to lay down a marker for the future, he had already promised John Smith he wouldn't stand against him. Both Brown and Blair considered standing for deputy leader, but Smith wanted Margaret Beckett as his deputy and Brown and Blair had no interest in standing for a post they could not win. As 'modernisers', the two should have supported Bryan Gould (who had Kinnock's support) but he was younger than Smith. If Gould won he was likely to be leader for a long time. Young and ambitious cardinals vote for old popes, and Smith and Beckett were elected.

Blair became Shadow Home Secretary, an important post that enabled him to have a truly national profile for the first time. He and Gordon Brown coined the slogan, *tough on crime, tough on the causes of crime*, a sound bite which brilliantly encapsulated the core of 'caring Thatcherism'. Blair was also cultivating support for the future. People were beginning to notice his charisma.

Tough on crime, tough on the causes of crime.

BLAIR

On television especially he seemed relaxed yet authoritative, as he was later to put it himself, a *regular sort of guy*. Both men and women liked him and Bryan Gould's place as the modernisers' choice to replace Smith was usurped; Gould soon left politics altogether for academic life in his native New Zealand.

Blair's performances at Labour Party conferences were less impressive than his television appearances. In 1990 he made his first major conference speech and he stumbled over his words and was clearly nervous. He was not a natural Labour Party man and conferences then were rather different affairs to the stage-managed homogeneity of today; even now his conference appearances are sweaty and unconvincing performances.

Given Blair's association with the modernising of the party, and his and Brown's undisputed position as heads of the modernising faction during John Smith's leadership, it is important to remember that Smith was responsible for ending the trade union block vote, where one trade union leader would cast their individual members' votes as one block. This gave the unions enormous power over conference decisions and when electing leaders and selecting parliamentary candidates. Blair himself had benefited in Sedgefield from the TGWU's block vote. One member, one vote (OMOV) was pushed through by Smith against union and left-wing opposition. Notwithstanding Blair's greater support for OMOV, Smith regarded Brown as his protégé. Despite his birthplace, Blair was not part of what has been described as John Smith's Scottish Mafia and Smith found Brown more *simpatico*.

Early on 12 May 1994, John Smith died suddenly of a heart attack at his Barbican flat. The events immediately following his death are the subject of much spin and counter-spin and the 'truth' may never be known. As Beckett and Hencke put it, 'entire rainforests have been consumed' in attempts to understand what went on during those few crucial days.[2]

What is clear is that Gordon Brown thought he would be leader and remained unaware of Blair's ambitions until it was too late. The two men had agreed not to fight each other and Brown had always seen himself as the senior figure. Behind the public expressions of grief the battle for the leadership began immediately the news of Smith's death was announced. Apparently, the day began with Peter Mandelson saying it 'must be Brown' but by the end of the day he had swung over to Blair's camp. Brown supporters believe he had always intended to support Blair but Paul Routledge maintains Mandelson initially favoured Brown and switched to Blair relatively late, recognising his greater ability to connect with the public. Mandelson's friends, and despite the jibes he has them, told Anthony Seldon that despite his 'love' for Brown he appreciated the formidable political talents of Blair. Just three days later, and in support of Mandelson's instincts, a MORI poll delivered a further blow to Brown's chances. Blair was the clear favourite with the public as the next Labour leader while Brown trailed in fourth behind John Prescott and Margaret Beckett. The first episode of the satirical puppet show *Spitting Image* after Smith's death featured a school-uniformed Blair squeakily singing 'I'm going to be the leader'.[3]

The famous pact at the Granita restaurant in Islington, where it is alleged Blair agreed to resign as Prime Minister during his second term to make way for a Brown succession, is disputed. If Brown truly believed a Prime Minister would voluntarily resign in this way he is guilty of extraordinary naivety. Whatever happened, years of resentment were to follow from Brown and his supporters, creating an extraordinary rift in the heart of the Labour governments from 1997. The rift only began to be healed after the 2005 general election, when Brown's succession finally appeared imminent following Blair's decision not to contest another election as leader, and then it was only a brief truce. Brown has little doubt Peter Mandelson is to blame for the 1994 'stitch-up', another indication of Blair's extraordinary gift for deflecting criticism and opprobrium which might justly fall on his own shoulders.[4] Brown believes that while he was in Scotland mourning for an old friend, Mandelson (who wrote asking Brown to stand down) and Blair were plotting against him. Indeed, Mandelson's machinations were so unpopular with many of Blair's supporters that Blair was forced to agree Mandy would not be involved with his leadership campaign. Mandelson, of course, had a key role. Referred to by the code name of 'Bobby' it was not until after Blair's election that his participation became more widely known.

A deal was agreed; Brown would be Chancellor and have considerable discretion over domestic policy – a decision that was called a 'fatal error' by Blair's economic adviser[5] – while Blair would control foreign policy. Brown reluctantly agreed not to run for the leadership and on 21 June 1994 Tony Blair defeated Prescott and Beckett to become the 15th leader of the Labour Party. In what in retrospect seems an inspired move, the ticket was balanced with John Prescott as deputy leader. Prescott gave Blair links with the grassroots of the party, offering them reassurance that the modernising tendency would not stray too far from the heart of old Labour, while remaining sufficiently low-profile not to frighten the electorate. The campaign to ensure victory in 1997 began and nothing was to be left to chance.

Despite the introduction of OMOV, Blair had been impatient with Smith's reluctance to press ahead with internal change and suspicious of his friendliness with union bosses. Blair wasted little time in accelerating the 'modernisation' of the party. He replaced party secretary Larry Whitty, who was seen as too close to the unions, with Tom Sawyer, a committed Blairite. He proposed a new set of aims to replace a dated charter, particularly tackling Labour's long-term commitment to public ownership enshrined in Clause IV of the party's charter. The intention to kill off Clause IV was announced at the 1994 October conference with barely a whimper, the need to win office taking precedence over ancient shibboleths. A fifth general election defeat in a row was unthinkable.

Perhaps even more importantly for its public impact, the conference slogan 'New Labour, New Britain' marked a rebirth of the party. Old Labour was dead and new 'improved' Labour was finally here; Philip Gould's long desire to rebrand the party had finally found a supportive leader. Gould's book *The Unfinished Revolution*, subtitled 'How the modernisers saved the Labour Party' later helped to consolidate the idea that John Smith's party had been heading for defeat and eulogised both Blair and Mandelson. Smith's tactics for electoral success were contemptuously dismissed as 'one last heave'. The continued use of the title 'New Labour' effectively drew a line under what had gone before and the institutional changes supported the contention that the old Labour Party was dead and buried. Philip Gould called the decision to abandon Clause IV a 'symbolic shock' that liberated the party.[6]

Blair sought rapprochement with big business and the largely Conservative press. An avalanche of 'personal' articles appeared in all sections of the press, stressing his moderation and his desire not to upset the achievements of Margaret Thatcher. He assured the Confederation of British Industries (CBI) in a private meeting that he would have to sign the

European Social Chapter giving workers extended rights and protections as it was a party commitment but that further proposals would be subject to CBI approval.

Blair's desire to take no chances extended to an astonishing pact with the Liberal Democrats. In his desire to realign centre-left politics, Blair had set up a working party on proportional representation. He had long planned to bring the Liberal Democrats into any future Labour government; his meetings with their leader Paddy Ashdown began (secretly, of course) even before Blair became leader. Two Cabinet seats were to be reserved for Liberal Democrats after a successful election but the size of Blair's majority ended the plan.[7]

He successfully wooed the British press. His famous meeting with Rupert Murdoch in which the media mogul promised the *Sun*'s support – strangely, at the same time Blair started to take a more liberal view of the cross-media ownership Murdoch was campaigning for – further demonstrated the determination to take no chances. The *Sun*'s support was probably unnecessary for victory but the message that Labour really was new and improved was reinforced to the paper's ten-million plus readers. Perhaps more crucially, he persuaded the *Daily Mail* to take a less hostile approach; many of the middle-class upwardly mobile voters he needed to impress were *Mail* readers. The Excalibur 'instant rebuttal' computer system was installed at Labour headquarters in Millbank Tower. This massive data base of government speeches, policy statements and general pronouncements could be utilised to effectively counteract or point out the inconsistencies in Tory statements within hours and sometimes minutes, enabling Labour to counter any Conservative spin and turn the story into 'government confusion'.

All of this preparation must not be allowed to mask what now tends to be forgotten. Blair was then extraordinarily attractive to and popular with the public. The journalist and editor Dominic Lawson (not a man easily impressed) recalls dining out with the young Labour leader and the stir his appearance in the restaurant caused was beyond Lawson's experience.[8] Those who met him personally remarked upon his political dynamism and charisma and his television appearances captured public imagination. A young family man, he appeared refreshingly normal when contrasted with John Major's government. Recognising his appeal, Mandelson ensured the party political broadcasts and campaign literature focused on him to an unprecedented extent. Tony Blair *was* New Labour. As Andrew Rawnsley notes, Blair was made leader on the sole basis that he would deliver power – 'win the first time, or you're out'. Therefore, he dominated the party's messages in an unprecedented way. The leadership demanded that decision-making power be centralised around a small team and stressed the need for tight discipline and adherence to the party line from MPs. Dissenters, however minor, were warned not to give the press any chance to refer back to the dark days of Labour splits or it could lose the election. Given this, it is inevitable that New Labour's election campaign would be essentially cautious.

The Conservative campaign spent a fortune (£13 million compared to Labour's £7 million) without any effect on the opinion polls. The Saatchi's golden touch had deserted them. Devised by the new M&C Saatchi agency, the infamous 'New Labour, New Danger' campaign with its motif of Blair's 'demon eyes', was risible. No one believed that a socialist monster lurked behind Tony Blair's exterior.

In an age where old ideological certainties had been questioned and in the case of Eastern European communism were dead and gone, New Labour was a party that appeared largely unencumbered by ideological baggage. For those who cared, the party proposed a 'Third Way'. Popular with Bill Clinton, it had been tailored for New Labour by the eminent sociologist and LSE director Anthony Giddens as a commitment to social democracy. For Blair, to all intents and purposes, the doctrine proposed a commitment to public-private partnerships in the pursuit of policy objectives. Essentially, the Third Way was adopted as a pragmatic 'ideology' for a pragmatic party where neither the state nor the market had primacy or a monopoly on solutions. What mattered was what worked, rather than a commitment to any one form of service delivery such as nationalisation or market solutions. The Third Way appeared the perfect ideology for a post-ideological age.[9] Labour's election theme song – 'Things Can Only Get Better' – sent a message that change would be gradual rather than revolutionary, a message the electorate were happy to hear.

The Conservatives were dogged by allegations of sleaze and corruption. Accordingly, 'trust' became a key theme of Blair's public pronouncements, contrasting him with a government that nobody trusted anymore. Labour won an astonishing landslide victory (beyond all the predictions) with a majority of 179 seats. Aged 43, Tony Blair was the youngest Prime Minister since Lord Liverpool in 1812. The youthfully jubilant and distinctly 'un-British' celebrations (as we now know, carefully stage-managed) that greeted Blair's arrival at Number 10 promised a new type of government led by a new kind of politician. It did not take long for such optimism to begin to be dashed.

Part Two

THE LEADERSHIP

Chapter 5: Blair's First Term: an Opportunity Lost

The new government's first act on taking office was to give the Bank of England the power to set base interest rates. Previous governments had routinely manipulated interest rates for political gain just before elections and Brown's decision sent out an immediate message – 'we really are different from previous governments'. At the same time however, new Labour MPs were dismayed to be told that policy was to be secondary to the primary goal of achieving a second term. Right from the start, safety first became the watchword. While Blair had promised voters change would be evolutionary rather than revolutionary, very little progress towards key aims seemed to be being made. Doubters were reassured that the second term would deliver the radical policies in health, education and social reform that would transform British society and leave a lasting legacy. But fear of a return to the electoral wilderness meant nothing must be allowed to prejudice winning that historic second full term, a lack of boldness Blair was later to regret.

One area where the government initially appeared radical was in constitutional reform. But what seemed at first to be a major series of constitutional reforms has largely disappointed. While some of the changes have been major they have also been incoherent, effectively creating an even more confusing system than before. For example, in devolution, a Welsh Assembly and Scottish Parliament were set up with vastly different powers and with different electoral systems; yet regional assemblies for England, a logical step, failed to materialise. Blair briefly favoured directly elected mayors for English cities, apparently in the belief that all around the country numbers of 'mini-me' mayors would be elected. Very few cities adopted the idea, but where they did Labour lost a number of strongholds, including Middlesborough and Stoke-on-Trent, to independent mayors. The Greater London Authority came into existence in 2000 and Blair's candidate for London's first directly elected mayor, Frank Dobson, was humiliatingly defeated by 'Red Ken' Livingstone, long-time foe of the modernisers. More importantly, as most councils decided against a mayoral option, the changes created further confusion in the already arcane system of local government Blair had inherited.

The House of Lords was reformed, ending the rights of hereditary peers to sit. The relative lack of protest at the ending of hundreds of years of tradition provides a salutary indication of just what Blair could have achieved in a number of policy areas if he had only been bolder. Instead, the Lords reforms were piecemeal and uncertain and the chamber's final form is no clearer now than it was in 1999. A number of key decisions were taken which ensured as tight a hold as possible on backbenchers. For example, Prime Minister's Questions on Tuesday and Thursday were replaced by one Wednesday session and the sitting time of Parliament was reduced, further limiting the already limited ability of Parliament to scrutinise both the PM and his legislation.

Despite manifesto commitments to reduce class sizes in schools, a number of policy decisions raised concern about the government's commitment to 'education, education,

education'. In higher education, very quickly and without warning in the manifesto, student grants were replaced by repayable loans; in Blair's second term, top-up fees for universities were introduced despite a manifesto commitment not to, although to soften the blow grants were reintroduced for students from very poor backgrounds. In primary and secondary education there was some success in improving exam results, reducing some class sizes in primary schools, the creation of specialist schools, and the introduction of literacy and numeracy strategies at primary level. Despite this, concern about poor standards of educational attainment continued.

There were some clear early successes. The introduction of a minimum wage greatly helped both young and low wage earners, although there was criticism that fear of a negative response from business had led the government to set the minimum wage too low. A long list of targets was set for public services and some of them were met. One major criticism was that pressure to meet targets resulted in resources moving to meet easily measurable outputs; for example, in the NHS, meeting centrally-set targets on reducing waiting times was at the expense of other and arguably more important aspects of patient care.

In Northern Ireland, initial optimism that the Good Friday

One area in which there has been major change under Blair has been that of lesbian and gay equality. After a prolonged struggle with the House of Lords, the age of consent for gay men was equalised at 16 in 2001. This was followed by the lifting of the ban on gays serving in the military after a decision in the European Court, the repeal of Section 28, and reform of the criminal law to remove any distinction between heterosexual and homosexual offences. In 2005, the government introduced registered civil partnerships for same-sex couples.

Agreement of 1998 (when most parties in the Troubles, including the Irish government, agreed on a democratic framework to share power) would lead to a solution were disappointed in 2002 when the new assembly was suspended and direct rule once more imposed. Although terrorist activity has largely ceased, the 'Troubles' still await a permanent solution, but Blair deserves credit for continuing the initiative for peace begun by John Major's government.

Blair had expressed the wish that he wanted to change British attitudes towards the European Union, although he has had to acknowledge his failure. Before his election in 1997 he announced at a lunch with staff of the Eurosceptic *Spectator* that he was determined to join the Single Currency and end the 'ambiguous relationship' Britain had with Europe.[1] In 1997, the Treasury had set five 'economic' tests for joining the Euro. The UK economy needed to 'converge' with the Euro-zone economy so that Britain could cope with Euro-zone interest rates; business and the workforce must demonstrate 'the ability to adjust to change'; a decision needed to be made on whether joining the European Monetary Union (EMU) would encourage investment in UK business; joining must not adversely affect the UK financial services industry; and what the Treasury called the 'fundamental test', that growth stability and employment would be promoted long-term.[2]

All in all, a sense of an opportunity lost pervades Tony Blair's first term. Few people were worse off, some were better off, but his commitment to Tory spending plans, seen as essential to convince Britain that the state was not going to be extended further and that they could trust New Labour, limited his policy options. Other events, both the tragic and the scandalous, were to cast the first shadows on Camelot.

The death of Diana, Princess of Wales, in the early hours of 31 August 1997 was a huge shock to the country. Blair was

Blair and Europe

In his 1996 'vision' for Britain, Tony Blair promised to deliver 'leadership and confidence' in Europe.

Before his election in 1997, Blair told the Eurosceptic *Spectator* that he was determined to join the single currency and end the 'ambiguous relationship' Britain had with Europe. Privately, he also assured the CBI that although he would have to sign the European Social Chapter giving workers extended rights and protections as it was a party commitment, further proposals would be subject to CBI approval.

In 1997, Blair and Gordon Brown set five 'economic' tests for joining the Euro. The UK economy needed to 'converge' with the Euro-zone economy so that Britain could cope with Euro-zone interest rates; business and the workforce had to demonstrate 'the ability to adjust to change'; a decision needed to be made on whether joining EMU would encourage investment in UK business; joining must not adversely affect the UK financial services industry; and the 'fundamental test', that growth, stability and employment would be promoted long-term. The five tests were almost entirely subjective, effectively giving Gordon Brown and the Treasury a veto on any decision. By the spring of 2003, the Treasury had decided the five tests for joining the euro had not been satisfied and that the euro-zone economies were not matching the UK's growth. Polls showed increasing public opposition to the euro, an omen Blair could not ignore.

Just before the 2005 general election, Blair told Sky News that while the political case might be strong the economic tests had not been met and it was unlikely that a referendum would be held before the 2009/10 election. His six-month presidency of the EU in 2005 hoped to achieve a 'fundamental review' of the EU's objectives and economic performance. Despite some successes, he failed to deliver on this; Chatham House gave him 'two cheers' for a competent but uninspirational tenure.

Tony Blair has often expressed the wish to reconcile the British people to Europe and change their attitudes towards the European Union. He has had to acknowledge his failure to achieve this.

at his constituency home when he got the news and immediately realised the impact the news would have on Diana's adoring public. When Blair arrived at his Trimdon church later that Sunday morning, Michael Brunson of ITN asked him if he had anything to say. Blair spoke of his shock and sorrow and eulogised the dead woman as if she were a saint, concluding with a phrase suggested by Campbell that: *She was the people's princess and that is how she will stay, how she will remain in our hearts and our memories for ever.*[3] Although the phrase was not original, Alastair Campbell's suggestion of the 'people's princess', quickly taken up by the media, demonstrates an essential cynicism at the heart of the government's actions. Sorrow was not allowed to intrude on the construction of a memorable soundbite for the PM.

Neither the Spencer family nor the Royal Family wanted a big funeral but Blair, with the support of Prince Charles, successfully argued that the public's clear wish to pay their last respects to a much-loved public figure must be considered. Unlike Blair, the Queen had badly misjudged the public mood. Newspaper criticism of her apparently cool attitude to Diana's death, including her refusal to fly the Buckingham Palace flag at half-mast, had fanned public outrage at the Royal Family's treatment of Diana. Blair delicately but clearly represented such views to the Queen. Shocked by the public response to her actions, and advised by Blair and Alastair Campbell, she was effectively forced to make a television statement and fly the flag at half-mast. The funeral, which included a mawkish version of *Candle in the Wind* performed by Elton John, saw an unprecedented outbreak of open public grief as Diana's coffin made

She [Diana] *was the people's princess and that is how she will stay, how she will remain in our hearts and our memories for ever.*

BLAIR

a very public journey to her family home, Althorp in Northamptonshire. It is doubtful that the Royal Family was grateful for Blair and Campbell's interjections, even though their advice saved the family from considerable public criticism. When the Queen Mother died in 2002 the Palace took great steps to prevent Blair from 'taking over' her funeral in the way they felt he had hijacked Diana's.

Tony Blair and his government had a longer than usual honeymoon period in office. Governments are now lucky to get more than a few weeks grace before the attacks start. Arguably, the media felt that they themselves had some culpability in the extraordinary fall in public trust and confidence in our elected politicians during the Major years. Blair's personal opinion poll ratings were generally positive. It would be absurd to portray the New Labour government as riddled with corruption, but there were soon to be lapses of judgement and questionable decision-making. Within just six months of gaining office, the squeaky-clean image had been tarnished.

Although Blair's first honours list in August, rewarding donors and fundraisers, had raised some predictable taunts of 'Tony's Cronies', the first major blow to the public's trust in Tony Blair came in November 1997. It emerged that Bernie Eccleston, the diminutive boss of Formula One motor racing, had donated £1 million to the Labour Party just before they came into power. Ecclestone said there was 'no question' that his donation had been in order to influence the next government to exempt Formula One from the ban on tobacco advertising, but few believed him. Since the election, Labour's health team had been adamant that all tobacco advertising, including sponsorship, would be banned. Ecclestone sought and got a private audience with Blair and attempted to convince him of the damage to jobs if Formula One was forced to locate its headquarters elsewhere.[4] An exemption for the sport followed, but with no similar judgement for darts and snooker, both also heavily reliant on tobacco sponsorship. The government's obfuscation and disingenuousness during and after this 'crisis' were early signs that New Labour politicians might be little different to all other politicians. On the *Today* programme, Gordon Brown failed to be completely honest about the donation and told his chief spin doctor Charlie Whelan: 'I lied. I lied. My credibility will be in shreds. I lied. If this gets out I'll be destroyed.'[5] Peter Mandelson, then Minister without Portfolio, admitted the government had behaved 'out of character' and might have appeared to 'stall and hide'.[6] Most commentators were blunter in their assessment. The advice the government sought from the Chairman of the Commission on Standards in Public Life, Sir Patrick Neill, was unwanted; he advised the donation should be returned to avoid even the appearance of donations for policy influence. Forced to defend himself publicly under television cross-examination by John Humphrys, Blair came up with a statement that has returned to haunt him. Asserting that he would never do anything improper, he said: *I think most people who have dealt with me think that I am a pretty straight sort of guy.*[7]

I think most people who have dealt with me think that I am a pretty straight sort of guy.

BLAIR

Blair's biggest early blow was the loss of one of the main architects of New Labour. Peter Mandelson was forced to resign as Secretary of State for Trade & Industry just before Christmas 1998, followed hours later by the Paymaster General, Geoffrey Robinson. A manuscript of Paul Routledge's biography of Mandelson had been leaked to the *Guardian*. Routledge had discovered details of a secret loan of £373,000 from Geoffrey Robinson, with which Mandelson had purchased an up-market flat in Notting Hill. Mandelson was less than honest about the circumstances surrounding the loan and had misled his building society, not to mention the parliamentary standards committee. Mandelson admitted that he should have declared the loan, especially as his department was investigating alleged irregularities in Robinson's private business affairs. The stench (real or not) of corruption meant both men had to go.[8] Mandelson's resignation was greeted at the Red Lion pub by Charlie Whelan with a champagne toast to celebrate his enemy's fall.[9] However, Tony Blair let the public know in the final paragraph of his published reply to Mandelson's resignation letter that his stay in the wilderness would not be long: *in the future, you will achieve much, much more with us*, said Blair and within the year he brought Mandelson back into the Cabinet as Northern Ireland Secretary in place of Mo Mowlam. Astonishingly, after riding out claims by Geoffrey Robinson that he had solicited the loan,[10] Mandelson was forced to quit again in January 2001 over allegations that he had improperly interceded over a passport application for the businessmen and Millennium Dome supporters, the Hinduja brothers. None of this unsavoury past prevented Blair from eventually appointing Mandelson as Trade Commissioner to the EU in 2004.

In the midst of such financial scandals, sexual sleaze returned to the agenda. Welsh Secretary Ron Davies' nocturnal stroll on Clapham Common ended with him being robbed of his wallet and car in Brixton by Rastafarians. Forced to resign for a 'serious lapse of judgement', the *Sun* led the next day with 'Cabinet Minister Quits in Gay Sex Scandal'. Earlier in his first term, Blair was informed that the *News of the World* was preparing to publish details of an affair between Robin Cook and his assistant, Gaynor Regan. On his way to a riding holiday in Colorado with his wife Margaret, the Foreign Secretary was contacted at Heathrow Airport by the PM's office and effectively told that if he wanted his political career to continue he must choose, immediately, between the two women: 'we want a decision', said Alastair Campbell. In Terminal Four's VIP lounge, Margaret was humiliatingly told that their marriage was over. Given that Campbell only did what he was told by Tony, it is interesting to get an insight into a committed Christian's regard for the sanctity of marriage. Months of damaging publicity followed for Cook and by inference the government as Cook's wife Margaret opened up their marriage to the British press and talked of Blair and Peter Mandelson's attempts to get her to keep quiet about the affair. She saw Blair as being more concerned with damping the media frenzy than with the collapse of her marriage.[11]

There was some good news for Tony and Cherie. On the day before the Labour Party conference in Bournemouth in the autumn of 1999, Cherie told her husband that she was pregnant with their fourth child. The media were told the news came as a 'total shock' to both of them. Named after his grandfather, baby Leo was born the following May, just nine months after the family holiday in France and Italy.

Amid this good news, there were more embarrassing events for Blair. Three years into his premiership, he was barracked at the Wembley Arena while addressing the Women's Institute (WI). His speech (rarely, mostly written by Blair himself) had been heavily criticised by Philip Gould for lacking conviction and following Blair's by now familiar path of mouthing platitudes specifically designed for the particular audience, in this case the *Telegraph* and *Mail*-reading women of Middle England. Despite Gould's concerns about platitudes, the WI members apparently resented receiving a blatantly 'political' speech when something less polemical was called for. Cruelly referred to by some as Blair's 'Ceausescu moment',[12] the WI's response seemed to capture a swing against New Labour in the popular mood. Oasis songwriter Noel Gallagher, who had once helped anoint Blair as the political epitome of cool Britannia, joined in the general chorus of disapproval at his government, vowing never to go back to Number 10. Charter 88 accused his government of creating an 'executive dictatorship' beyond Margaret Thatcher's wildest dreams. Even trade union leader and Blair loyalist Bill Morris accused the government of pandering to racists in its hostility towards asylum seekers, as New Labour sought a favourable press in the right-wing tabloids.[13] Increasingly, there seemed little difference between one departed group of old grey politicians and the new group of slightly younger, slightly less grey politicians.

In opposition, Blair had tried to reposition New Labour as strong on defence issues, one of Old Labour's weakest areas. He had been especially gung-ho in his condemnation of Saddam Hussein and Iraq. When Saddam expelled United Nations (UN) weapons inspectors, US President Bill Clinton had wanted to use air strikes; like Blair, Clinton was convinced that Saddam possessed weapons of mass destruction (WMDs). The UN Secretary General Kofi Annan persuaded Iraq to allow inspections to resume,

> On 21 December 1989 the Romanian dictator Nicolae Ceausescu was booed by the crowd assembled in Bucharest's main square for what was intended to be a 'spontaneous movement of support' for him. Ceausescu's bewilderment and inability to control the crowd was one of the defining moments in the collapse of Communism in Eastern Europe. An uprising followed, and Ceausescu and his wife attempted to flee, but they were both captured, tried before a military tribunal and shot on Christmas Day 1989.

but when in 1998 Saddam again expelled the inspectors, the US and Britain threatened air strikes if co-operation was not resumed. The UN and the rest of the Security Council disagreed but following an intense period of news management by Alastair Campbell, involving both British and American media, 'Operation Desert Fox' initiated four days of air attacks. Although the operation received a largely positive media response, there were accusations that the attacks were designed to turn attention away from the Monica Lewinsky scandal. More than one US source dubbed it 'Monica's War'. Both Clinton and Blair maintained the attacks had slowed down Saddam's weapons programme.

A number of features of 'Desert Fox' were to resonate. A small 'war cabinet' took the decisions and the Cabinet defence committee authorised those decisions, with the full Cabinet largely quiescent; roughly the same *ad hoc* structure would be adopted in future conflicts. The apparent success of the operation also gave Blair confidence that he was morally right and that bold action would be rewarded. Crucially, the conflict had also given proof of Mandelson and Campbell's beliefs about the importance of news management. In short, winning the war was only part of the battle; in the messy world of modern mediated politics where public perceptions were crucial, winning the *media* war was just as important. Helping New Labour in that war was a close team of insiders who effectively formed a largely unelected inner cabinet.

Chapter 6: In the Court of King Anthony

There is more rumour about the close relationships around Tony Blair's premiership than there is reliable information. Number 10 has been compared to a medieval court, where courtiers intrigue and compete for the leader's ear. No doubt all high political office is similar. Certainly Harold Wilson's 'kitchen cabinet' shared similarities but Campbell and Co. took such activities to new levels. It is difficult to believe that the level of backbiting in Blair's court has been conducive to effective government.

As his biographers have noted, Blair is in many ways the sum of the relationships around him. All his closest associates possess qualities essential to his political career and all of them have given more to him than the normal boundaries of professional relationship would dictate. Whatever else may be said about Blair, he has generated extraordinary loyalty from his close associates. As many have noted, Blair's charisma is not merely endowed by office; their loyalty to Blair began before he realistically had a sniff of the power and patronage he now possesses. It may sound 'Caplinish', but Blair has been fortunate (and clever enough) to have been surrounded by people who love him. Any examination of Blair's government needs to acknowledge the powerful role played by a small team of largely unelected advisers and friends, who congregated in 'the den', Blair's small office in Number 10, where many key decisions were taken away from Cabinet and the senior career civil servants.[1]

Peter Mandelson is a major architect of the New Labour brand with a deserved reputation for Machiavellian manoeuvring, although it has been of little use in preventing his own public disgraces ousting him from office. He is not loved in the party; Gordon Brown's chief aide Ed Balls once described him as 'the canker at the heart of the Labour Party',[2] a sentiment many share.

'The canker at the heart of the Labour Party.'

Despite Mandelson's initial preference for Gordon Brown as leader he quickly realised the qualities Blair possessed that made him an ideal face for the brand. Mandelson typifies the loyalty Blair engenders in his supporters and Blair's respect and affection for him is indicated by his successful rehabilitation to high office on two occasions and his survival in high office on other occasions when dropping him was an option. Like Blair, and despite being the grandson of Herbert Morrison, Home Secretary in Churchill's wartime coalition and Attlee's Deputy Prime Minister, Mandelson has little commitment to traditional Labour values. The author was present when Mandelson was asked by a congregation of political scientists at Durham University in 1990 if there were any Labour policies he would not be prepared to drop for the sake of winning an election: he answered simply 'no'.[3] Mandelson was the perfect Svengali for an ambitious and ideology-lite politician in a fast-changing political environment. Mandelson's commitment to the pseudo-ideology/philosophy of the Third Way was, despite the rhetoric, not shared for long by Blair once in government. However, the vague social democratic ideas of the Third Way favoured by Mandelson have permeated Blair's policies. That said, Mandelson's central value to Blair has been as an emotional rock. In the deepest sense of the word, and without meaning to launch a cheap shot, the two men love each other. Blair has described Mandelson as 'the keeper of his moods and feelings' and their relationship is endorsed by Cherie, who is also fond of Mandelson. When 'Cheriegate' threatened to destroy the trust Tony and Cherie shared, they turned to Peter for help and support. Mandelson told Anthony Seldon in 2003 that 'I'm always there for him'.[4]

Mandelson was a master strategist, but in terms of day-to-day dealings with the British press the down-to-earth Alastair Campbell provided a capable complement to Mandelson's more silky skills. From 1987, as political editor of first the *Sunday Mirror* and then the *Daily Mirror*, Campbell had a direct line to Peter Mandelson. Campbell was lined up to be Prime Minister Neil Kinnock's press secretary but election defeat in 1992 and John Smith's elevation appeared to have ended such hopes: Smith was no fan of either Mandelson or Campbell. Tony Blair's modernising project appealed to Campbell. As his closeness to the future Prime Minister grew, his relationship with Gordon Brown deteriorated. Initially seeing Brown as a future Prime Minister with Blair as his Chancellor, Campbell became increasingly enamoured of Blair and, along with his partner Fiona Millar (who became Cherie's minder in the early years of power) became convinced Brown was too 'idiosyncratic' to be Prime Minister.[5] On the day John Smith died, Campbell has said he knew Blair would be the leader and also knew that he would work for him; that night on *Newsnight* he was the one of the first people to declare publicly that Blair should be the new leader. Four months later he became the party's chief press spokesman.

Between 1994 and 1997 he prepared Blair for office and contributed to New Labour's media strategy. In office, Tony

Blair's closeness to Alastair Campbell intensified and he had a major role in the communication of the New Labour message. With the exception of Cherie, no one had more regular and privileged contact with Blair than Campbell. To his admirers, his energy, ability and loyalty to Tony Blair made him indispensable. To his detractors he was a yob and a bully, a chief contributor to the increasing cynicism of the British media and a man who encouraged Blair to concentrate on spin rather than substance.[6] Campbell is credited with enormous influence although Beckett and Hencke may have hit the nail on the head when they point out that perhaps the truest thing Campbell has said about his role at the centre of government is that, 'everything I do, I do because the prime minister wants me to'.[7] As with Margaret Thatcher's press officer Bernard Ingham, Campbell's power came because he really did speak with the Prime Minister's voice. Blair put him in charge of Strategy and Communications after the 2001 election.

'Everything I do, I do because the prime minister wants me to.'

ALASTAIR CAMPBELL

Unless *everyone* who has written about Tony Blair and his government is lying, there is no doubt about one aspect of Campbell's personality. He would threaten and abuse in the crudest terms anyone who he felt had 'fucked up'. Everyone in Number 10, including Tony and Cherie, felt the force of his bullying on occasion. Civil servants were not immune; Blair had given Campbell the authority to issue direct instructions to civil servants, a prerogative previously of ministers alone. Oborne and Walters' forensic and scathing examination of Campbell reveals a man whose bullying seems to mask a deep insecurity.[8] His need to serve and become attached to a strong master is apparent throughout his career and he famously punched the *Guardian*'s Michael White when he made light of the death of Campbell's former employer, the fraudster and would-be media mogul Robert Maxwell. He has also had drink problems and at least one nervous breakdown, not at first glance the ideal *curriculum vitae* for a prime ministerial aide, but he has been extraordinarily loyal to Tony. Like Mandelson, the dislike Campbell engenders allowed 'Teflon Tony' to survive relatively unscathed and it is astonishing how many people fail to understand that Campbell was only doing exactly what Tony wanted him to do. Alastair Campbell would not have survived as long otherwise.

For Anthony Seldon, without Campbell and Mandelson, whom he calls 'masters in their field', Blair would never have become the 'figure he did'.[9] Will Hutton, whose ideas on 'stakeholding' briefly became popular with Blair, has said that at key moments in Kosovo and the Northern Ireland talks, Campbell became a *de facto* deputy prime minister.[10] It's also important to note that whenever Blair needed to chill out for an hour or so, it was usually Campbell's company that he sought.

In 1998, during the fallout from the Ron Davies scandal, the ex-Conservative MP Matthew Parris 'outed' Peter Mandelson as being gay on the BBC TV programme *Newsnight*. This led to BBC management banning any mention of Mandelson's private life on air, a ban cheerfully flouted by the satirical quiz show *Have I Got News for You*. It is likely that Parris did not think he was saying anything that was not common knowledge, as some years previously the *Sunday People* newspaper had run an article on Mandelson's private life.

Campbell left government in September 2003 and his subsequent career has not been without its problems – for example, his disastrous stint as press officer with the unsuccessful British Lions rugby tour of New Zealand, where he alienated players and press, did his reputation no good – and although he kept in regular contact with Blair he clearly missed the day-to-day involvement in high politics.[11] He was eventually brought back into Number 10 by Blair, ostensibly to help ease the handover of power from a Blair to a Brown administration, although Charlie Whelan has dismissed as laughable the idea that the despised Campbell was advising Brown on anything.[12]

As Campbell complemented Mandelson, so Anji Hunter's 'silver-tongued' relationships with the broadsheet press, media owners and editors complemented Campbell's more visceral rapport with political journalists.[13] At the most intimate and personal level, none of Blair's inner court has been as close to him as Anji Hunter. It was Hunter who convinced the neophyte politician Blair that he could make it to the top and her support, encouragement and deep friendship was vital to his self-belief. She has been important to him almost throughout his political career and was a key player in selling the New Labour project to business leaders and the chattering classes. They first met at a party when she was 15 and Blair 17 and their times up at Oxford overlapped for two years. A sympathetic listener in the weeks after his mother's death, they kept in touch and she joined him as a part-time researcher in 1986. She became his closest adviser in Downing Street and her power included the ability to make or break the careers of junior ministers; Blair's ignorance of the talent in his party was apparently considerable and he relied on Hunter to keep him informed.

Hunter's ex-flatmate Sue Nye ran Gordon Brown's private office and their friendship helped to smooth over troubled waters on many occasions. However, Hunter, despite or perhaps because of her professionalism and considerable ability, was not especially popular with the Downing Street women. None of Blair's professional relationships has caused as much friction between him and Cherie as his long association with Hunter. Cherie, who perhaps hoped to emulate Hillary Clinton's powerful role behind Bill, was jealous of Anji's greater political closeness to Tony. Cherie's suspicion at the nature of the Tony–Anji relationship is well documented and stories abound of unpleasant confrontations between the two women; that Hunter's husband was a 'dead ringer' for Tony Blair did little to ease the tension.[14] Whatever the truth, Cherie was overjoyed when Hunter finally left after the 2001 election to take a well-paid job with the oil company BP. As well as her troubles with Cherie, Hunter frequently clashed with Sally Morgan, Blair's political secretary, and especially with Fiona Millar, which made Hunter's generally good professional interaction with Alastair Campbell a little tricky at times. One insider described the Campbell-Hunter relationship as 'love-hate', perhaps because Campbell's essential dealings with Hunter had to be necessarily circumspect. But Hunter was highly respected by mandarins, politicians and the media. Her importance to Blair is evidenced by the desperate efforts he made to get her to reject BP's generous offer, despite Cherie's anger at his desire to keep Hunter by his side. Sally Morgan, a Labour Party stalwart sent to the Lords by Blair, came back to take over Hunter's duties.[15]

Philip Gould is New Labour's pollster and focus group guru. While the focus-group findings which supported his arguments for Labour's 'modernisation' have been dismissed as unscientific for making huge generalisations without statistical support and his book *The Unfinished Revolution* is also accused of rewriting history to extol the genius and vision of Blair and Mandelson,[16] others see him as a 'brilliant strategist', unique in British political history. No one in any party, says Anthony Seldon, has ever had the 'continuity of influence' of Gould on a party 'he helped to create'.[17] Like the rest of the inner circle he is 'fixated' on Blair but, uniquely, he has remained relatively close to Brown, despite his focus groups and polls contributing to the decision that it had to be Blair. After John Smith's death, his privileged place within the circle rested on one key issue, his claim to tell Blair what the public were thinking; three election victories are taken as proof that he has succeeded in that mission. He is also not afraid to tell Blair unpleasant 'truths'; if he had been listened to the barracking by WI members might not have occurred. Jon Cruddas, now a Labour MP, was formerly deputy political secretary at Number 10, and believes that focus group discussions and the preferences of swing voters were given far too much weight by Blair.[18] Seldon argues this is misplaced concern and that the focus-group findings have essentially reinforced decisions Blair wanted to take anyway. That is, Gould's findings tend to support Blair's gut instincts.

Jonathan Powell's beliefs also tended to reinforce Blair's. The youngest of four sons, Jonathan is not the first Powell to be at the centre of government. His eldest brother Charles was Margaret Thatcher's most trusted civil servant and also served under John Major; in another sign of the small world of New Labour networks, Charles' wife Carla is a close friend of Peter Mandelson. Powell's second oldest brother Chris has handled Labour's advertising account and was an important figure in the Shadow Communications Agency, as well as being chairman of the influential think-tank the Institute for Public Policy Research. When Jonathan was First Secretary in Britain's Washington Embassy he became very close to Bill Clinton's team of advisers, absorbing some of the 'Third Way' rhetoric of Clinton's administration. As leader, Blair appointed Powell as, in American parlance, his 'chief of staff'. In office, he effectively became one of the Prime Minister's right-hand men and Will Hutton has described him sitting outside Blair's office 'driving policy'.[19] He was influential in the Good Friday agreement and a member of the war cabinet on Afghanistan, Iraq and Kosovo. His 'Atlanticism' – few people know more about American politics than him – reinforced Blair's. 'Devoted' to Tony Blair, Powell is an immensely able man who thought alike to Blair on key issues. This is not necessarily a good thing.[20] He was too often an echo when perhaps Blair needed someone who would make him think again. Julia Langdon, biographer of the late Mo Mowlam, called him 'the Downing Street poisoner' for his key role in governmental sackings and promotions.[21] After 2001, Powell became Head of Policy and by the 2005 election he was, along with Philip Gould, one of the few senior survivors of those who came into government with Blair in 1997.

Not all the key insiders at Number 10 are political figures. Carole Caplin's connection and influence with both the Blairs is at a much more personal level, as Cheriegate (see Chapter 9) vividly showed. The former glamour model first met Cherie at a fitness class in 1992 and by 2003 she was being paid £3,500 a month by Cherie for advice on lifestyle and 'earning every penny'.[22] She is almost as close to Tony as she is to Cherie, giving him the pet name 'Toblerone'. She frequently kept him company at the Downing Street flat when Cherie was away and also gave him 'reiki massages' to relive his stress, indications of just how much Cherie trusts her. And of how much Cherie also trusts her husband, of course; Caplin is a very attractive woman. That Carole Caplin has stayed close to Number 10 despite the problems over Cheriegate and the vitriol sprayed her way by Alastair Campbell and Fiona Millar indicates her importance to the Blairs. In the early days of power, Millar gave important advice to Cherie on her relations with the media and she had almost total control over access to Cherie. Millar had ruled Cherie with the proverbial rod of iron. She finally quit over her resentment at Caplin's increasing influence over Cherie in everything from her underwear to her spiritual development, although the reason Millar gave was to spend more time with her children and develop her own media career. She has become a successful journalist, specialising in education. Even in office, Millar had publicly criticised aspects of Labour's education policies,[23] and her commitment to comprehensive education has ensured her opposition to Blair's education reform bill.

There are a number of other people who have been important to Blair inside Number 10. Bill Bush, the former head of research at Number 10, like most of Blair's associates remains remarkably loyal to him. Geoff Mulgan, erstwhile director of the think tank *Demos*, became head of policy at Downing Street and is another loyal supporter. David Miliband, a rare 'intellectual' at the heart of Blair's government, was the principal author of the 1997 election manifesto, head of the Number 10 Policy Unit and particularly influential in a quiet way, especially on matters relating to the United States.[24]

Derry Irvine, Blair's old head of chambers, is one of those key people who 'hardened him into a capable and ambitious leader'. Blair once said Irvine, like Marvin the Paranoid Android from the cult BBC radio show *The Hitchhiker's Guide to the Galaxy*, had *a brain the size of a planet*, and there is no one whose judgement he had more respect for in his early leadership days.[25] His closeness to the Blair family is shown by them asking him to be godfather to their son Nicholas. Blair made him Lord Chancellor and trusted Irvine to chair more Cabinet committees than any other appointment. Despite Irvine's intelligence, he never developed his political antennae, and his public profile has been largely confined to a perception of him as gaffe-prone and rather pompous. His selection of antique wallpaper when redecorating his offices, costing £650,000, generated much negative press. He was finally dropped from government in June 2003; his value to Blair had been in those early days when Blair needed support and guidance.

Around the time he first met Cherie, Blair had been re-acquainted with a friend from his youth in Edinburgh, Charlie Falconer, also working as a barrister in adjacent chambers. Falconer was already a Labour Party activist and the two moved into a Wandsworth flat together. Falconer was to become a life-long and loyal friend and Blair made him both a peer and his first Solicitor General in 1997. Falconer and his wife are close friends of the Blairs and Seldon has remarked on how alike Falconer and Blair are, 'lifelong friends and soulmates'.[26] Falconer's advance under Blair provides further evidence, if any were needed, of the importance Blair has placed on trust and loyalty when making his key appointments.

Despite this, or perhaps because they were all competing for Tony's love, the relationships between the courtiers were often tense. The account of life with the Blairs given in Oborne & Walters' disrespectful biography of Alastair Campbell is cheekily paraphrased by Beckett and Hencke as a storyboard from a *Girls' Own* comic book. As with any close-knit group of people there are bound to be problems but it appears that the backbiting between Blair's courtiers often went far beyond what could be regarded as normal infighting. However, the account given by Oborne and Walters is flawed for Beckett and Hencke by falling into the same trap as other portrayals of Number 10. Whenever anything dishonest or eccentric is uncovered, it is always someone else's fault – the Machi-avellian Mandelson, the thuggish Campbell, the capricious Cherie – and Tony is always blameless. This helps explain why Teflon Tony's non-stick coating survived so long. Even his beloved wife's reputation during 'Cheriegate' was 'thrown to the wolves' to protect Tony.[27]

The decision-making relationship between the chief protagonists was carried on in an extremely casual manner for the heart of government. Lord Butler's report on the build-up to the Iraq war strongly criticised what he referred to as 'sofa style' government; that is, making important decisions while casually sitting around drinking coffee or lounging around the corridors of Number 10.[28] Blair's indifference to Cabinet government has been frequently remarked upon; Cabinet meetings were perfunctory and Blair preferred to meet ministers on a one-to-one basis. Blair kept a tight hold on policy initiatives from ministers and Miliband's Policy Unit closely scrutinised and often 'transformed' policy papers from government departments.[29] Geoff Mulgan has said that 'vested interests' from outside (and inside) sometimes exercised a 'malign influence' on policy. Mulgan also alleges that the knowledge Campbell was keeping a diary that he was planning to publish inhibited the frank exchange of views between colleagues and was 'corrosive to the quality of decision-making'. The consideration of alternative perspectives was inevitably limited by the fear that positing radical or controversial proposals could come back to haunt the proposer in a few years time.[30]

One key relationship at the centre of government deserves a short chapter of its own. Rarely have two men so concentrated two separate spheres of power within government, and a prime minister and his or her chancellor have never been so in opposition to each other as Tony Blair and Gordon Brown have been for virtually all New Labour's time in office.

Chapter 7: 'Gordon and Tony were lovers ...'

Blair's relationship with his Chancellor has aroused concern inside and outside of Number 10. At times, there has seemed to be a state of civil war between them, with both sides leaking the most appalling and vitriolic statements. Even after a rapprochement in 2005, when Brown was finally convinced Blair was planning to leave office, the fragile truce was broken following the allegations of secret loans for peerages that surfaced early in 2006. As allegations of sleaze mounted and the heat on Blair intensified, loyal Blairites accused Brown and his supporters of fanning the flames in order to destabilise Blair and force him out of office early. The accusations 'unleashed a firestorm of toxic briefing from both camps'.[1] Even allowing for tabloid exaggeration, the Brown-Blair 'partnership' was clearly scraping new lows and the desire for an 'orderly transition' of the leadership looked increasingly unlikely to be fulfilled.

The story of Brown and Blair reads a little like the old blues song *Frankie and Johnny*: 'he was his man, but he done him wrong.' They had shared an office in Parliament and dreams for the future. With the arrival in 1986 of Peter Mandelson they became an inseparable trio, committed to modernisation. Brown and Blair were especially close in those years, good friends who enjoyed each other's company, but there were clear differences between the two. Brown's attitude to business people in particular, and capitalism in general, was markedly more antagonistic than Blair's. On the other hand, Brown's attitude to the trade unions was more positive. They also differed fundamentally on the merits of John Smith. Brown remained close to Smith, but Blair saw him as tainted by the corruption and cronyism of the party activists in his Monklands constituency.[2] Their recognition of the need for Labour to change, and crucially, that Brown would one day be the leader driving that change, was the essential core of the relationship.

It is astonishing how often the word 'love' is used to describe Blair's close relationships. A long-term Blair aide has described the regard Brown and Blair had for each other as exceptional, full of 'love' and 'human warmth'.[3] That personal and political closeness began to weaken from 1990, perhaps as Brown started to recognise that Blair's political ambitions rivalled his own. Their relationship, along with Brown's friendship with Peter Mandelson, was finally fractured by Brown's realisation after John Smith's death that Blair had usurped his position as heir presumptive to the Labour crown.[4] It was a difficult readjustment for him, as for so long he had been Blair's mentor and unquestionably the senior figure. Brown believed Blair had reneged on their agreement that Blair would support a Brown leadership bid. However, the opinion polls failed to support Brown's candidature and Brown appears to be fooling himself that his impact could have been comparable to Blair's.[5] Committed to the modernisation project and aware that any hint of a rift would play into a right-wing dominated press's hands, they enjoyed an uneasy 'marriage of convenience' which turned into a 'cold war' once Labour won.[6] Paul Routledge's 1998 biography of Brown, written with the Chancellor's full co-operation, contrasted Brown's dignified mourning after Smith's death with Blair's political manoeuvrings.[7] The book further contributed to the frostiness, exacerbated when Routledge's unflattering biography of Mandelson appeared the following year.[8] Alastair Campbell's assertion that 'no prime minister and chancellor have ever had a closer or more productive relationship'[9] is just not true. Campbell's insistence that Blair got on very well with Gordon and his staff is challenged every time a journalist speaks to Charlie Whelan. When Campbell's diaries are finally published we'll hopefully get something a little closer to the truth about the Blair-Brown feud.

'No prime minister and chancellor have ever had a closer or more productive relationship.'

ALASTAIR CAMPBELL

Even very early on in power the feud was well established. Following his speech in Blackpool to the party conference of 1998, Brown, Ed Balls and Charlie Whelan, off to an International Monetary Fund meeting in Washington, were being driven to Manchester airport by a local party activist. As they listened to Blair's conference address, Brown's mood gradually darkened as the applause grew for what he believed were primarily his achievements, and he kept up a running heckle throughout Blair's oration.[10] Blair's one-time economics adviser, Derek Scott, has revealed that Number 10 was often unaware of the details of the Budget until shortly before their delivery and alleges that Brown was more likely to reveal such details to journalists than to Number 10.[11] Brown's office responded by accusing Scott of 'the deliberate peddling of lies and distortions'.[12] With Brown's full support, Robert Peston's 'self-serving' and distorted account of recent political history has presented Blair as incompetent and untrustworthy.[13] With what Bowers regards as a typical lack of nerve from the Chancellor, as the fallout from Peston's book spread

Brown dismissed the revelations as 'unreliable gossip', despite those revelations being couched in Brown's own words. Bower argues this demeaned Brown and undermined faith in the Chancellor's own 'veracity and principles'.[14]

Of course, there is another side to the argument. It could be said that the Chancellor and his Treasury team were important in providing Blair with essential opposition missing from a supine Cabinet, by raising 'informed questions that no one else dared to ask'.[15] However, attempts by some of his supporters to portray Gordon as the representative from the traditional core of the party and Tony as the moderniser fail to acknowledge that some of Brown's own polices have upset the left, such as cutting benefits to the disabled. Brown, as his liaison with Blair and Mandelson in those heady days when they were instrumental in establishing the need for change shows, is quite clearly a central partner of the New Labour project although it now suits his ambitions to be seen as a bastion of traditional values.

Brown's attitude to Number 10 is starkly revealed by his actions after Geoffrey Robinson's resignation over the Mandelson home loan scandal. Brown had vehemently opposed the decision to force Robinson's resignation[16] and blaming the messenger rather than the source, he refused to speak to the Cabinet Secretary Richard Wilson for three years, an unbelievable piece of childishness from the Chancellor.[17]

Quite a few attempts have been made to end their damaging feud. Gavyn Davies, erstwhile Chairman of the BBC, husband of Sue Nye, and one of the few people then trusted by both Blair and Brown, hosted a 'ceasefire meeting' in January 1999 between Brown and Mandelson. Blair had decided that the feud must end[18] but the rift was too wide. By the spring of 2001, his opinion poll approval rating of 65 per cent supported the *Daily Telegraph*'s description of him as 'the most popular chancellor since the war',[19] only serving to heighten Brown's sense of grievance and make Blair even more suspicious of him. Brown's importance to the New Labour project was clear, but his resentment grew. The 2001 election was characterised by bad blood between the two men; Blair did not speak to Brown until five days after the historic victory. Numerous petty or thoughtless acts have fuelled Brown's resentment. For example, on 6 January 2005, Brown was furious when Downing Street rescheduled Blair's monthly press conference for 10 a.m., the precise time that Brown's long-planned speech on aid to Africa and the developing world was being delivered.[20]

But it is in his simmering resentment at the failure of Blair to hand over office to him that Brown most closely reveals his true feelings. The true nature of the discussions in 1994 at the Granita restaurant will never be established, but it is clear that Brown truly believed he would succeed Blair sometime in Labour's second full term. Brown maintains that Blair confirmed in November 2003, over dinner at John Prescott's flat, that he would stand down before the next election. Eyewitnesses Anji Hunter, Peter Mandelson and Alastair Campbell have denied this, but in the immortal words of Mandy Rice-Davies, 'they would, wouldn't they'. In support of their denials, Brown's most recent biographer Tom Bowers doubts that Blair would ever have been so blatant.[21] In July 2004, again at a dinner in Prescott's flat, Blair told Brown that he was staying. Brown told close aides, who dutifully leaked it to the press, that he told Blair: 'there is nothing you can say to me now that I could ever believe'. Blair denies the exchange took place.[22] While recognising the difficulties of establishing what really

'There is nothing you can say to me now that I could ever believe.'

GORDON BROWN TO BLAIR

happened, Tom Bowers' biography of Brown raised serious doubts about his suitability for the highest office.

Of course, he may never get the premiership; if Charles Clarke has his way he never will and Clarke is not alone.[23] Brown wants Blair to go soon and polls suggest the public shares that wish,[24] but it is Blair who will probably decide his own leaving date. If a week is a long time in politics, then the wait for Blair to go could be a very long lifetime. Brown does not want to join Rab Butler, David Owen, Hugh Gaitskell and others on the select list of 'the best prime minister we never had'. A younger and more media-friendly rival may emerge from almost nowhere, as David Cameron did to take the Conservative leadership, and with every day that passes, the chance grows that, as Harold Macmillan famously put it, 'events, dear boy, events' will conspire to snatch the crown from him.

Chapter 8: International Statesman

Prior to the 1997 election much had been made of Robin Cook's declaration that Britain would pursue an 'ethical foreign policy'. Cook had been reformulating British foreign policy and stressing Labour's support for using military force when necessary and in 1998 events in Iraq demonstrated that this new toughness was not just rhetoric. In 1999, Kosovo would provide a clear test of the ethical foreign policy philosophy and provide further proof of Labour's tough stance on defence issues.

There is no space here to give anything but the briefest and inevitably inadequate summation of the complex background to the Kosovan conflict. Following the break-up of the Soviet Union and its satellites, the former Yugoslavia had witnessed numerous human rights abuses and war crimes, notably in Kosovo where Yugoslav President Slobodan Milosevic's Serbian army were slaughtering Muslims and committing further atrocities. Blair had raised the issue of the bloodshed in the former Yugoslavia many times in opposition, notably over massacres in Bosnia, and had forcibly criticised the Major government for its failure to act. Both Cook and Blair felt that the use of military force was now necessary.

Despite agreeing a ceasefire, Milosevic's troops continued their 'ethnic cleansing'. What followed was a classic example of the CNN effect; crudely, show a crisis on television, demand something must be done, and something is done.[1] Public pressure was mounting after TV pictures of mass graves and of the great hardship faced by Kosovan refugees were highlighted on programmes such as *Newsnight*. The Russian veto ensured that there would be no support from the UN for an air war but the Anglo-American coalition was determined to use force. In a foretaste of what was soon to come in Iraq, on 24 March 1999 the air attacks on Serbian targets began. It has been alleged that the main effect of the bombing was to provide cover for more ethnic cleansing and to unite the Serbs behind Milosevic. It also led to the massive movement of refugees and mounting international opposition to the bombing. Comparisons were being made with Suez and even Vietnam. Blair, especially angry at the BBC's coverage, told a senior aide, *this could be the end of me.*[2]

This could be the end of me.

BLAIR

Blair pressured the Americans, both directly in appeals to President Clinton and indirectly through a series of news leaks and articles by favoured journalists, to agree to send ground troops. Clinton was apparently furious at the briefings against US prevarication, which had Number 10's fingerprints all over them. Alastair Campbell had been sent to NATO to oversee their media management of the war. The British government produced a set of criteria for justifying intervention in international conflicts, with scant regard for either international law or the authority of the UN. The threat of ground troops and, perhaps more importantly, American pressure on Milosevic's Russian allies to help end the crisis, finally led Milosevic to back down and NATO stopped the bombing.

Blair's statement after the Serbians signed a peace agreement on 9 June was messianic in its tone: *Good has triumphed over evil; Justice has overcome barbarism. And the values of civilisa-*

tion have prevailed.[3] But what was supposed to have been a short, sharp war lasted 78 days (a warning for the future that was ignored) and Kosovo became a long-term drain on NATO resources. In the aftermath of 'victory' Russian forces occupied Kosovo's main airport and only prudent action by British commanders prevented an American over-reaction which would have greatly escalated the conflict. A year later Milosevic was removed by his own people and finally died of a heart attack in 2006 while awaiting trial at The Hague for war crimes.

Whatever reservations one may have about some of the actions, Blair's intervention certainly saved lives and prevented a further escalation of the conflict. Whether it was the humanitarian triumph the spin machine attempted to portray is another matter, as ethnic cleansing continued even after the peace agreement. But Blair won many admirers for his resolute decision making on Kosovo and the crisis established him as an international figure. Rawnsley admires Blair's articulation of the ethical basis for intervention and contrasts his actions with the 'weaselly equivocation' of other Western leaders. For Rawnsley, 'a man most often portrayed as a skilled opportunist exposed the moral, stubborn, zealous dimensions of his character'.[4] For others too, it was the finest moment of his premiership. It was also a career high-point for Defence Secretary George Robertson. His high profile over Kosovo was a significant factor in his appointment later that year as NATO Secretary-General.

Blair's Kosovan experience convinced him that he had a major role as the 'bridge between the United States and Europe' and was uniquely qualified to 'explain the one to the other'. Blair, somewhat isolated in both his government and in the Western alliance, was taken to the 'brink of his self-belief' and trusting on his instincts and his certainty that

The Special Relationship

Britain has long thought of itself as especially close to the US, joined as we are by a common language and sharing many cultural and political values. The 'special relationship' was enshrined by Roosevelt and Churchill's friendship during the Second World War when US isolationism was no longer feasible. There have been a number of frissons in the relationship, notably America's lack of support for Britain during Suez, its failure to give unequivocal support during the Falklands crisis and Harold Wilson's refusal to support America in Vietnam, which soured relations between him and Lyndon Johnson.

For critics, Britain's position is subservient and the 'special relationship' is only special for America when its own interests are served. Many American politicians, including Bill Clinton, despite his friendship with the Blairs, have been sceptical of the concept. In truth, America has a number of other 'special relationships', most notably with Israel, Canada and Mexico. For most Americans, the phrase has no specific connection with Britain.

Personal relations – Thatcher and Reagan formed a mutual admiration society – are the key to a productive 'special relationship'. Blair has had close relations with two American presidents. His association with George W Bush was initially cold, but Blair's dash to Bush's side following 9/11 and his decision to support American intervention around the globe, most notably in Afghanistan and Iraq, led to a much closer personal relationship.

However, Britain has hardly been 'rewarded' for such loyalty. Most contracts to rebuild Iraq have gone to American firms with White House links and Blair failed to persuade Bush to sign the Kyoto Agreement in 2005. Later that year came further embarrassment for Blair, when Congress refused to accept there was such a thing as a special Anglo-American accord and denied privileged access to US defence technologies for Britain. This was despite warnings that a failure to grant this privilege would be a serious blow to the 'special relationship'. The legacy of Iraq and the estrangement that decision caused with our European partners are heavy prices to pay for Blair's commitment to the special relationship.

his actions were right, Kosovo also increased his faith in his intimate circle of friends and advisers and bolstered his sense of his own certainty.[5] Such feelings are not always beneficial to Caesars. Blair's sense of his own rightness, whatever the circumstances, was to lead to actions in Iraq that have blighted his premiership and seriously damaged his reputation for probity.

However, in domestic politics, the immediate repercussions of his Kosovan triumph were less positive. Following poor local and European election results in 1999, the government attempted to put a positive gloss on its defeats. John Prescott maintained the poor turnout represented 'a culture of contentment', in that voters were so happy with the government that they didn't feel the need to vote. Philip Gould's focus groups had warned him that the Kosovo conflict was doing Blair damage at home. He was starting to be seen as someone more concerned with sorting out other people's problems than sorting out Britain's and Gould and other pollsters reported disappointment among Labour voters at the lack of progress in education and health. Despite such concerns, Philip Gould told Blair to ignore public opinion polls on his actions on Kosovo, telling the Prime Minister that 'the only important thing is to win'.[6] But such polls were reflecting growing concerns within the British electorate that New Labour had yet to deliver on its promises.

'The only important thing is to win.'
PHILIP GOULD

As the next election approached, there was a reminder that 'events' could upset the best-laid plans. The fuel crisis of 2000, with oil refineries blockaded by hauliers and farmers angry at high fuel taxes, raised the spectre of the dark days of the 1970s and briefly battered Labour's opinion poll ratings. Blair handled the dispute personally, firmly telling the oil companies that he would institute emergency procedures unless they got their tankers moving. The dispute ended without Blair making any concessions, but it was soon to be followed by a much bigger problem for farmers than high fuel taxes when an unprecedented outbreak of foot-and-mouth disease hit Britain just before the general election.

Despite such problems, there was never any danger of electoral defeat. New Labour had proved it could rule without economic catastrophe and Blair was still popular. Although there were the usual warnings to the troops against complacency, Blair and New Labour went into the 2001 general election assured of victory. Although the government had failed to meet two of its 'five pledges' made in 1997 (cutting class sizes for infants and fast-track punishment for young offenders, which were met by 2002) it had met nearly 80 per cent of its 229 manifesto promises.[7] While it had failed to deliver on some key promises, such as reducing street crime, and while the value of some of those pledges is debatable, this was on the surface an impressive performance.

Campaigning on general themes of improvement in public services (especially the NHS) another landslide majority of 165 seats was delivered. Turnout was a concern; less than 60 per cent of those registered bothered to vote, heading down towards American levels of engagement in national elections. Pundits ascribed the low turnout to the apparent inevitability of Blair's victory; perhaps, but the fall also demonstrated increasing public apathy and distaste for modern party politics. The Conservative campaign was lacklustre. Despite the issue's lack of resonance with voters, Conservative electoral messages concentrated on opposition to British membership of EMU. No one expected them to win, including themselves, and William Hague resigned as leader the morning after the election defeat.

Blair's second spell in government was to be dominated by the so-called 'War on Terror'. But there were some important domestic events, not least 'Cheriegate'. Policy-wise, tax rises allowed increasing spending on health and education and the Foundation Hospitals scheme was introduced to give hospitals greater financial freedom; however, most additional funds were swallowed up by pay rises.

The election itself was straddled by a major crisis for British farming when a foot-and-mouth epidemic challenged the government's ability at crisis management. The worst outbreak of the disease in the world in recent times, it is estimated to have cost the British economy £6 billion. As it was the first significant outbreak of the disease since 1967, the government could hardly be held solely responsible for the lack of a contingency plan, but it was widely criticised for its confused and muddled approach. After a brief but critical delay in banning animal movements by the Ministry of Agriculture, Blair quickly took charge of policy but took advice almost solely from the scientific community, effectively ignoring the opinions of interested parties such as farmers and veterinary surgeons. Over six million animals (most of them healthy) were culled; the Ministry later admitted that a policy of selective

In the 20th century Austen Chamberlain (1863–1937) had held the distinction of being the only Conservative Party leader (March 1921 to October 1922) never to be Prime Minister, but since then he has been joined by William Hague, defeated in the 2001 election, Hague's successor Iain Duncan-Smith who lost a vote of confidence of Conservative MPs in November 2003, and Michael Howard, who stood down after defeat in the May 2005 general election. David Cameron, seen as the Tories' answer to Blair, is the fourth Leader of the Opposition Blair has faced across the Dispatch Box.

vaccination should have been followed. The spectacle of huge pyres of dead animals had a disastrous impact on the sale of British food and on local economies dependent on tourism and provided an unwelcome backdrop to the 2001 election for Tony Blair.[8] However, his approval rating and the party's opinion poll lead were barely dented. Given the apparent eradication of foot-and-mouth, the government might even claim that culling was, despite the criticisms, the right policy to pursue.

Perhaps the worst tactical decision Blair made, and one he later admitted was a mistake,[9] was to announce in October 2004 that he would not seek a fourth term. He had an example close to home which should have warned him about this in Sir Alex Ferguson, a key New Labour supporter honoured by Blair. Ferguson's announcement that he would retire at the end of the 2002 premiership season led to huge problems within Manchester United. By the time Sir Alex did his famous u-turn and decided to stay, the atmosphere between him and key players like David Beckham had become poisonous. Inevitably, it's difficult to maintain discipline if the troops know you won't be there much longer. Equally inevitably, although Blair had said he would stay for a full term, speculation began about when he would go. Backbenchers who now knew their political careers were unlikely to be decided by Blair were given more licence to be bolshy.

Inevitably, the events of 11 September 2001 dominated Blair's second term. The attacks, which demolished the World Trade Center and damaged the heart of the American defence system, the Pentagon, were played out to a spellbound and horrified western audience on prime-time television. At some other places in the world – Afghanistan and Palestine, for instance – there were uninhibited scenes of joy that America's mainland had been attacked. Immediately, Blair's message was one of uncompromising support for his American ally.

War in Kosovo had established Blair as a major international figure. War in Iraq was to blight his international reputation, with the exception of within the United States, permanently. The Iraq war and its immediate consequences will be examined in Chapter 10.

,

Chapter 9: Religion and Family

Blair's religion is central to his and his family's lives. His father's stroke in 1964 which ended Leo's very real ambitions in Conservative politics was obviously a significant event for Blair, yet the glib assertion that the 11-year-old Blair's political ambitions began then, as his father's ended, is unconvincing.[1] Friends at school, and later in his pop entrepreneurial hiatus between Fettes and University, are united in remembering an essentially apolitical young man. Blair's obsession was for success in the rock business, either as performer or promoter; his adventures with Ugly Rumours while at Oxford indicate that even by then greater exposure to political ideas had not blunted his desire to emulate his hero Mick Jagger. Nor was it an especially key moment in the development of his individual faith. While his father's death affected Blair spiritually it was not until his undergraduate years that his faith was cemented by his discussions with Peter Thomson.

Parts of the rock-star lifestyle appear to have been out of bounds to young Tony. Astonishingly, it appears beyond dispute that, unlike his compatriot Bill Clinton, Blair never puffed a marijuana cigarette, yet alone inhaled the smoke. Although he has admitted allowing his father-in-law to smoke a joint in front of him one of the first times they met,[2] John Rentoul's cross-examination of old friends and casual acquaintances leaves little room for doubt. Given the appeal of a Jaggeresque role-model and the probable degree of peer pressure this reveals considerable powers of self-control for a young undergraduate. A central reason for this failure to experiment must be his religious beliefs.

Blair's Christianity is an essential and, until his third term of office, a remarkably under-considered aspect of his life. A failure to recognise the centrality of Christianity to Tony Blair's life has generally been a characteristic of most press coverage. Given the media's general failure to assess this aspect, public ignorance of this facet of Blair was not surprising. Although his biographers noted his religion's importance to his personal philosophy, it was only very late in his premiership that his religion came to wider public knowledge, and it was Blair who put it there. Questioned about his actions on Iraq on Michael Parkinson's chat show, he solemnly told Parkinson that God would be his judge. Asked by Parkinson whether he would pray to God when making such a decision, Blair responded *I don't want to get into something like that*.[3]

Such pronouncements are potentially dangerous in the secular world of British politics. Alastair Campbell has tried to prevent Blair discussing religion ever since 1996 when a *Telegraph* interview had raised some controversy. Behind the scenes, Blair's religion was a potential factor in all his decision-making. Cherie Blair told her partners at Matrix Chambers that every night during the Iraq conflict Tony knelt by his bedside and prayed. Sir Peter Stothard, former editor of the *Times*, alleged that while waiting to deliver his television broadcast to the nation on the eve of the 2003 Iraq war, Blair announced that he wanted to end the broadcast with *God Bless You*. After protests from all his staff, the phrase was not used and the broadcast ended with *Thank You*. Blair was also alleged to have said that he was ready to *meet his Maker* and account for his decision to go to war in Iraq.[4]

Given that Bush's every pronouncement seems to include the description 'born-again', that Blair's policy decisions (especially on Iraq) have rarely been connected to his fundamental Christian, essentially Catholic, beliefs is strange. Perhaps the only explanation is that the 'conventional' religious beliefs of public figures are not considered a suitable area for investigation by the media. If Blair had been a Scientologist it is fair to assume that the press would have drawn connections between his beliefs and his actions. Certainly, a contributing factor to the small part Christianity has played in his public persona until very recently, is the 'instinct for secrecy' which appears to grip Blair and his 'court'.[5] In response to claims made in an American study of President George W Bush, when asked by Jeremy Paxman whether he had prayed with Bush at Camp David, Blair testily denied it. In an interview with *Vanity Fair*'s David Margolick, Blair was asked whether his faith 'bonded him' to Bush and whether he had discussed religion with President Bush. Blair replied: *I can't say it's something we've discussed, but it's something we share.* Alastair Campbell intervened and said; 'I'm sorry. We don't do God.'[6] Blair's remarks on *Parkinson* have ensured that his religious beliefs will now be fair game for wide discussion.

'I'm sorry. We don't do God.'
ALASTAIR CAMPBELL

Blair also doesn't do 'family' – except, of course when it suits his purposes. Party political broadcasts prior to the 1997 general election made considerable play of the family man, even to the extent of including discussions with his children. Blair, mug of tea in hand, was shown at home with his children; watching Euan doing his homework Blair joked: *Homework? You wait until David Blunkett gets in. You'll have plenty of homework then.*[7] Unusually for a Prime Minister's family, Tony, Cherie and their four children, Euan, Nicholas, Kathryn and Leo, do not live at 10 Downing Street but next door at Number 11, traditional home of the Chancellor. The private accommodation there is bigger although the family is still cramped, especially after Leo arrived. Gordon Brown has occupied the small flat above Number 10. Tony Blair is the focus of 24-hour media attention and that media spotlight has inevitably created the odd problem or two. Blair has said that his children cope with having a Prime Minister for a father because once the door is closed they *become a normal family* with housework, homework and the daily routine: *I think if your family is very strong ... touch wood it works,* he told Michael Parkinson.[8] It is difficult not to sympathise with a family that has to live in such a goldfish-bowl atmosphere but the whole Blair approach to the media regarding his family has been characterised by a certain schizophrenia.

Blair's frequent resentment at media intrusion demonstrated a lack of understanding of the game. To coin a cliché, when you sup with the devil, you need to use a long spoon. He's prepared to admit that despite being no good with technology, he has an iPod that he relies on daughter Kathryn to download to, and that, surprisingly for an old rocker, Christina Aguilera is on his iPod. The birth of Leo in May 2000 was, cynics might suggest, used as evidence to the electorate of Blair's continuing virility and a source of positive photo opportunities. Leo toured the world providing plentiful human-interest story lines, meeting everyone from the Queen at Balmoral to Bill Clinton at a UN summit in New York. There were complaints about invasion of privacy when unauthorised pictures of Leo appeared in the press despite strong representations by the Blairs not to publish them. In response, pictures of Leo and the family were made available to any publication on payment of £500 to Cherie's favourite cancer charities. You can't use your young family for publicity purposes and then expect your political decisions on family matters not to be connected to your family decisions in the same areas. To be fair, most prime ministers have not entered high office with such a young family; Blair has had to chart a difficult course between satisfying public curiosity and protecting his family's privacy.

Leo was inadvertently to cause political embarrassment to his dad. In 2001, because of public concerns about its links with autism, the take-up of the triple vaccine MMR (measles, mumps and rubella) was nearing dangerously low levels and the government was urging the nation to trust its scientists who said such concern was misplaced. Blair would not say whether Leo had received the triple vaccine or individual vaccines; despite a claim that this was of legitimate public interest, he refused to discuss the health issues of his children. While sympathising with this stance, the issue quite clearly raised important questions in the public interest, as did the decision to send the ten-year-old Euan halfway across the capital to the grant-maintained London Oratory school in Fulham. It aroused press accusations of hypocrisy and considerable public and political indignation. Fiona Millar, fundamentally opposed to

The last 20th-century prime minister to have a young family at Number 10 was Asquith, whose daughter Elizabeth was 11 and son Anthony was five when their father came to office in 1908. Lloyd George's daughter Megan had lived at Number 11 when her father was Chancellor, and moved next door with him in 1916 at the age of 14. Ramsay MacDonald, Attlee, Wilson and Major's children were teenagers during their premierships, and Macmillan occasionally had his grandchildren staying with him at Number 10.

selective education, was furious; her later opposition to Blair's education reforms was no inconsistency. Alastair Campbell advised the Blairs of the likely press reaction and was allegedly so angry with the decision that he contemplated resignation. However, Blair was said to be happy with the message it sent out about the importance of parental choice.[9]

He was also happy to cite Euan as someone he consults to see how the younger generation feel about government policy and Euan's opinion was allegedly a key factor in deciding whether the exhibits in the Millennium Dome would appeal to families; the 'Euan factor' failed to prevent the Dome being a commercial and public relations disaster, perhaps because Peter Mandelson was almost solely responsible for deciding its contents. Euan's encounter with a Leicester Square gutter at the age of 16 has been well documented and provided his father with a more accurate insight into a young Briton's behaviour. Celebrating the end of his GCSEs, Euan was discovered by police vomiting on the pavement and taken into custody. It was especially embarrassing for his father because just a few days before Tony Blair had proposed giving the police powers to impose on-the-spot fines for drunken and disorderly behaviour. Given this, it was naïve not to expect considerable press coverage. It did give Blair the opportunity to show the caring family man when he spoke later that week about family and community values at a Faith in the Future conference in Brighton and told his audience: *Being a prime minister can be a tough job, being a parent is probably tougher, and sometimes you don't always succeed. But the family to me is more important than anything else.*[10] Euan's headmaster at the Oratory School took a tolerant view of the incident.

Chequers, the traditional country home of Prime Ministers, is very much the Blairs' weekend family home. Chequers is a splendid Elizabethan mansion in the Chiltern Hills near

Princes Risborough, Buckinghamshire, given to the nation by Lord Lee of Fareham in 1921. Set in over 1,000 acres of farmland and woods, and protected by high security, it is one of the few places where the Blairs can relax as a family out of the media's scrutiny. Children's bicycles lie around the place and there are football goalposts on the lawn. The Blairs, especially Cherie, love it there. Cherie gives apparently very well-informed guided tours for visitors and guests. Inevitably, many of their guests are on official business, such as President Chirac and President Clinton, but the Blairs appear to delight in inviting guests from show business, including Cilla Black, David Bowie and even Michael Winner. Mick Hucknall of Simply Red is a regular guest. Media personalities such as Anna Ford, Piers Morgan and Andrew Marr are also invited. Most dinner parties at Chequers comprise a mixture of such guests with perhaps a Cabinet minister and certainly one or more insiders. Guests are greeted by the housekeeper and served aperitifs by Royal Navy staff before being led into the spacious, wood-panelled dining room. Beckett and Hencke list the guests entertained by Tony and Cherie at one such dinner party in 1998; lawyer and novelist John Mortimer, whose *Rumpole of the Bailey* books were popular with fellow lawyer Cherie, accompanied by his wife Penny; Philip Gould and his publisher wife; John Smith's widow Elisabeth and one of her daughters; the Channel 4 news reporter Sarah Smith; Gerry Robinson from Granada TV, one of Blair's biggest business supporters and a major donor to New Labour; Cherie's mum Gale; and Robin Cook with his new wife Gaynor.[11]

Few of their family affairs have aroused as much criticism as their choice of summer holidays. They have holidayed in luxury. Veteran pop singer Cliff Richard's home in Barbados, Italian media magnate and politician Silvio Berlusconi's Sardinian estate and Geoffrey Robinson's Tuscany villa (whose three-storied mansion has been called a palace) are just a few of the retreats they have enjoyed thanks to the courtesy of rich friends. Of course, we all like to take advantage of friends' generosity, but the propriety of accepting some of these invitations for an elected politician with huge powers of patronage should have been more closely considered.

Despite Euan's drunken escapade, the family member who has caused Tony Blair most problems with the media is Cherie. Unlike their children, as a semi-public figure herself, she's seen as fair game. She was captured by photographers answering the door of their Islington house on the first

Being a prime minister can be a tough job, being a parent is probably tougher, and sometimes you don't always succeed.

BLAIR

morning of a new Labour government, looking as all of us do after a busy night. The nasty press she received for her dishevelled appearance means that Cherie has been rightly suspicious of the media's intentions towards her. In January 2000, she was on her way by train from Blackfriars to Luton to sit as a Recorder at Luton Crown Court. Without sufficient cash for the ticket machine and unable to use her credit card, she was caught travelling without a ticket and fined £10.[12] The idea that she had been deliberately evading payment is absurd yet the British press enjoyed putting the knife in; not suffering fools gladly, and not bothering to hide it, Cherie has not been popular with journalists.

Cherie's dabbling with 'new age' gurus and medicine, and her long association and friendship with Carole Caplin, generated much press ridicule and was to create unprecedented problems inside the Blair marriage. In December 2002 Cherie suffered her most unpleasant intrusion at the hands of the British media. For the Blairs and their friends the scandal, inevitably dubbed 'Cheriegate', was a cooked-up affair mostly fanned by the *Daily Mail*'s coverage, while for their critics it was further evidence of their essential unfitness for public office. At Cherie's request, Carole Caplin viewed two Bristol flats in preparation for Euan's time at the University of Bristol. One flat would be for Euan; the other was to be an investment for the future. None of this was illegal or remotely improper, although an apparently casual ability to fork out considerable sums of money for two properties at once raised some eyebrows. Unfortunately for the Blairs, Caplin's then partner Peter Foster, a convicted fraudster the press had already run negative articles about, was involved with negotiations over the purchase and subsequently boasted to business associates about his closeness to the Blairs, claiming to be their financial adviser. The *Mail on Sunday* ran the story and, after checking with Cherie, Alastair Campbell and the Number 10 Press Office issued a quick rebuttal of Foster's claims. Campbell was furious when the *Daily Mail* revealed that Foster had indeed negotiated on Cherie's behalf and that e-mails from her to him confirmed this.

Campbell and his partner Fiona Millar were no friends of Carole Caplin, who had largely usurped Millar's role as chief confidante to Cherie; Campbell was known to refer to Caplin as 'that bloody woman'.[13] Campbell had lied to the press, and this time he thought he had been telling them the truth – his already shaky reputation for veracity was further tarnished. The briefing in the press against Cherie that followed reflected his anger. Stories appeared rubbishing her reliance on Caplin and ridiculing her belief in New Age rituals. In turn, Caplin and Foster briefed against members of the inner court.

According to insiders, it was one of the blackest moments in Tony and Cherie's marriage. He had been misled and his faith in her had been damaged. It got worse when allegations, quickly denied, surfaced about Cherie interfering in attempts by the Australian government to extradite Foster. Desperate times require desperate measures and Peter Mandelson was called back from the United States to sort things out. Campbell and Millar argued that Cherie should say nothing, but Mandelson was convinced that she should make a public apology. Live on television from Millbank, she declared that she was not a Superwoman and that keeping so many balls in the air had contributed to her decision to allow someone she 'barely knew' to act for her in buying the flats. At Campbell's insistence she declared that she alone was responsible for 'any misunderstanding' between the Number 10 press office and the media. As usual, nothing must be allowed to damage Tony. Her strain throughout was evident and she appeared to come close to breaking down at times.[14] Media reaction to the speech varied from admiration for her courage to revulsion at the spectacle. Despite other 'revelations' emerging in the days afterwards, 'Cheriegate' gradually fizzled out. But the Blairs' reputation for probity was further damaged and their reputation for obfuscation and disingenuousness was enhanced. Fiona Millar's friendship with Cherie was severely damaged by the affair and they will never recapture their former intimacy. There was a sad postscript to the affair as Caplin, pregnant with Foster's baby, miscarried. Both Cherie and Carole blamed the stress of Cheriegate for this unfortunate event. The affair intensified the Blairs' dislike of media intrusion, which without doubt was higher than it had ever been. The strain of living almost constantly in the public eye was taking its toll. Following the 'scandal', there were persistent reports of Tony Blair also being enamoured by Caplin's beliefs. Her influence, it was alleged, even went so far as choosing the prime ministerial underpants.[15] Despite the trauma her association has cost the Blairs, she remains close friends with both of them.

Tony Blair has had a number of health problems that Caplin has sought to help alleviate, including a slipped disc, but his major health problem was beyond her capabilities. In October 2003 he received treatment for an irregular heartbeat and although he was back at work within 48 hours he eventually had to have an operation at Hammersmith Hospital to correct it a year later. Despite initial fears about his health affecting his capacity for office, and although he has clearly aged in office and sometimes looks tired, Blair has coped adequately with the pressures. His health appears to have held up well and he told Michael Parkinson that he had only failed to get a good night's sleep on three or four occasions since becoming Prime Minister.[16]

In 2005, Cherie was attracting further negative press. A series of talks in Australia for a children's cancer charity earned her more than £100,000 and it was alleged that only a small percentage of the proceeds went towards cancer research.[17] The majority of the British press relished the opportunity to portray Cherie as money-grabbing and hypocritical. Her well-publicised and profitable lecture tours generate a large amount of negative press coverage and she is accused of making money from her family connections. It is often overlooked that she is a well respected and successful barrister whose contributions to the family income have far exceeded her husband's and that her own entirely realistic high political ambitions were thwarted by her husband's great luck at meeting John Burton in Sedgefield.

In May 2004, intimate family problems involving one of his children which the British media agreed not to report led to rumours that he would soon resign; Blair apparently felt that his family were being unfairly exposed to the pressures of life with the Prime Minister. Also, the continuing problems in Iraq were contributing to his depression.

However, his concern about leaving a permanent mark on history convinced him he would have to stay. If Iraq was to be an entry on the positive side of history's ledger he could not leave with the country in chaos. He 'no longer trusted Brown to entrench his legacy', in fact, 'quite the opposite' as the briefings against him by Brown's supporters continued. On the last day of the party's annual conference in September he announced his decision to fight the next election but not to seek a fourth election victory in 2009 or beyond.[18] Three of the key figures in his life had persuaded him to stay and fight. Peter Mandelson and Lord Falconer argued that he still had things to achieve. But the most important voice was Cherie's. Despite the family problems, and the public ignominy the media spotlight had brought her, she told him that he still had things to achieve and must stay in office.[19] As ever, Cherie put Tony's career first. Despite the odd embarrassment this otherwise independent and highly intelligent woman has caused him, he has been lucky in his choice of life partner.

Chapter 10: Iraq and the War on Terror

It is the actions Tony Blair took following the attacks on mainland America on 11 September 2001 ('9/11') which look set to constitute how he will be largely remembered, at least in the immediate future. The legacy his decisions have left – including a less safe Britain, virtual civil war in Iraq, and what amounts to almost a holy war between much of the West and the Muslim world – is unlikely to establish the reputation he has sought. From the time of the attacks to long after the occupation of Iraq by 'Coalition' forces, his and his government's conduct has been characterised by deceit, fabrication and misrepresentation. History's judgement is likely to be harsh.

Al-Qaeda, a terrorist group led by Osama Bin Laden and based in Afghanistan, admitted responsibility for the attacks on the World Trade Center and the Pentagon. It was probably only the bravery of doomed passengers on the fourth hijacked plane that prevented the White House being hit. In the immediate aftermath of 9/11, the Taliban in Afghanistan were given an ultimatum; either shut down the terrorist camps and hand over Osama Bin Laden or face military action. In order to bring Russia onside, or at least neutralise them, their razing of Chechnya would be accorded status as part of the 'war on terror', which given the bar- barities they committed in the former Soviet province is a somewhat chilling illustration of *realpolitik* and the moral relativism applied to the term 'terrorism'. Less than a month after 9/11, Britain and America attacked Afghanistan. The capital Kabul fell on 13 November and within a short time the first cargoes of chained and hooded prisoners, including British and American citizens, were being flown to Guantanamo Bay.[1] Many are still held prisoner in appalling conditions, denied even the right to know what they are charged with or given the chance to defend themselves in a court of law. The spectacle of the world's biggest propagandist for 'democracy' ignoring basic human rights by humiliating and torturing suspects must have been especially galling to the leading human rights lawyer Cherie Booth although, of course, she remained silent. Not until early in 2006 did Blair tentatively suggest the Guantanamo Bay camp should be closed.

President Bush's state of the union address in January 2002 named Iraq as part of an 'axis of evil'. Despite the fact that 15 of the 19 Al-Qaeda hijackers were Saudi Arabians and none were Iraqi citizens, and that many American commentators had accused the Saudis of funding Muslim militant groups,[2] Iraq's culpability for 9/11 was firmly established among most American people. While no one now bothers to deny the lie, Saddam Hussein was alleged by both Bush and Blair to have close links with Al-Qaeda. It very quickly became apparent to observers of American politics that regime change by invasion was the means favoured by Bush.[3] Publicly, Blair continued to promote the need for UN endorsement of any such action. Bob Woodward claims that privately Blair had assured Bush that if necessary he would commit British troops for military action, although Bush's closest advisers were still advising against attacking Iraq.[4] However, when the two men hosted a joint press conference in Texas in April it appeared to some observers that it was a matter of when, not if.[5]

His Iraq decision-making must have generated considerable heat in the Blair household; Cherie is not afraid to make her views known to her husband, although she has generally been remarkably discreet in public. Matrix Chambers, as specialists in human rights law, went public in its belief that invading Iraq would be contrary to international law. Cherie, again, was silent on the issue but it is inconceivable that her law firm would make this announcement without her knowledge and agreement and the statement probably expressed her own belief.

On 24 September 2002 the British government published a dossier which claimed that Iraq possessed weapons of mass destruction (WMDs) and that Iraqi forces could deploy biological or chemical weapons 'within 45 minutes of an order to do so'. Iraq was also alleged to be within one or two years of producing atomic weapons. The dossier, supposedly based on information compiled by the intelligence agencies, was presented as clear evidence of the need to take action against Iraq. Further government press releases made claims of human rights abuses against Saddam Hussein, with no acknowledgement that many of the worst atrocities had taken place when Iraq was an ally of the West and when Iran or Libya had been designated the 'axis of evil'.[6]

Relations between George W Bush and Blair could have got off to a bad start, given how close Blair had been to his Democrat predecessor Bill Clinton, but Blair's support of the 'War on Terror' and the invasion of Iraq has ensured that any awkwardness did not last. Before the 2005 election, the Conservative leader Michael Howard was snubbed by the US President for his attacks on Blair's Iraq policy. The President's advisor Karl Rove is alleged to have told Howard: 'You can forget about meeting the President. Don't bother coming.'

Saddam Hussein had allowed UN weapons inspectors back into Iraq, but as time went by and the inspection teams failed to find evidence of WMDs, Bush and Blair's impatience with the UN increased. A further briefing paper was issued in February 2003 in an attempt to put pressure on the UN to agree a second resolution approving military action. The dossier was quickly discovered to have been substantially compiled from an old PhD thesis available on the Web. The thesis had made certain hypotheses that the dossier portrayed as fact. This briefing paper, now known as the infamous 'Dodgy Dossier', had been 'sexed-up' to provide a stronger basis for military action and has done more to harm Blair than any other action. It established him as 'BLIAR' in the minds of opponents to the war and large anti-war protests indicated the degree of public discontent. The dodgy dossier was also to reverberate more tragically for others, who lost their jobs and in one case their life.

The late Robin Cook finally discovered his ethical foreign policy principles and resigned as Leader of the House. Overseas development minister Clare Short thought about resigning then thought again, and then finally resigned too late to have any impact, losing what little credibility she had left along the way. The Foreign Secretary who'd replaced Cook, Jack Straw, had proposed an ultimatum for the UN; unless Iraq fully complied with weapons inspections it would be invaded. China, France and Russia's opposition (President Putin was basically indifferent to Western opinion on his tactics in Chechnya) ensured there would be no such resolution. There was clearly no chance of the UN supporting invasion.

In a televised address to his nation on 18 March 2003, President Bush gave Saddam Hussein 48 hours to leave Iraq, knowing of course that he neither would nor could comply.

The assault on Iraq began two days later and was cased in apocalyptic language. The massive firepower used – the US described their tactics as 'shock and awe' – amounted to what was effectively 'airborne terrorism'[7] especially on beleaguered Baghdad. The assault on America's biggest city was being avenged, and that Iraq was not involved in the 9/11 attacks seemed not to matter. Three weeks into the war, Baghdad was conquered and the statues of Saddam began to tumble in what appeared spontaneous acts but were often carefully-orchestrated publicity exercises. There was great exultation from Downing Street and the White House that the war had been 'won' so easily and at such small cost to Coalition forces. Three years and more on, such premature triumphalism seems both hollow and obscene.

The inquest into Iraq had some unexpected and tragic consequences. In May 2003, in a very early morning broadcast for the *Today* programme, BBC reporter Andrew Gilligan said a senior source had told him the intelligence services were unhappy with the contents of the government's dossiers, especially the claim that WMDs could be launched in 45 minutes. Additionally, the source said the government 'probably knew' the claim was wrong but decided to put it in anyway. The report raised few eyebrows as by now everyone knew the claim was bogus, although Gilligan did not repeat his assertion that the government probably knew this in later broadcasts that morning. The incident might have passed, but a few days later, Gilligan wrote in the *Mail on Sunday* that it was Alastair Campbell who had 'sexed up' the 'Dodgy Dossier'. In fury, Campbell did the rounds of the media, demanding an apology from the BBC and that they reveal Gilligan's source. In the internal investigation that followed, Dr David Kelly, a senior government scientist and a member of the UN weapons inspection team, admitted to his bosses that he had talked to Gilligan. Shortly after, the Ministry of Defence confirmed Kelly's name as the source of Gilligan's story. Dr Kelly gave evidence to the parliamentary Intelligence and Security Committee on 15 July 2003; the next day he committed suicide. Opinion polls following Kelly's death found a decline in trust for Blair and a belief that his government was losing control of events.[8] Kelly's death effectively forced the government to set up an inquiry into whether the document had been 'sexed up' and into how his name had been leaked; on 1 August, the Hutton Inquiry officially opened.

In January 2004 the Hutton Report was published. Hutton completely exonerated Campbell and the government and found that Gilligan's allegations were 'unfounded'.[9] Following the report, which 'sprayed the government with more whitewash than a Costa Brava timeshare' according to Boris Johnson,[10] while castigating the BBC, a spineless Board of Governors effectively sacked their Chairman Gavyn Davies, and the Director-General Greg Dyke; Gilligan soon followed. David Kelly, of course, lost something more important than his job. So, despite the essential truthfulness of Gilligan's report, three key BBC figures lost their jobs while no one in government did.

The Hutton Report, with its narrow brief, failed to satisfy the important question of whether Blair had taken Britain to war on false premises and he was forced to set up another inquiry under Lord Butler to examine the quality of the intelligence information given to the government. Unsurprisingly, the Butler Report found that the sources of intelligence on Iraq and WMDs were unreliable. It also noted that Blair chaired a meeting on foreign and defence policy in July 2002, long before the Iraq war, at which Iraq's capabilities were noted to be smaller than other 'states of concern'.[11] However, while Butler was critical of some aspects of Blair's style of governing, he found, to the surprise of many interested observers that Blair had acted throughout in good faith.[12] Once again, the good old British political system delivered the goods. When there's a stink, set up an inquiry (or two), and it will be guaranteed to deliver a judgement that lets government off the hook. As Boris Johnson noted, Gilligan had 'an important, accurate and exclusive story' and whatever Hutton said, the 'facts' had been 'embellished' by Alastair Campbell. The government's claims were false and Britain went to war on 'what turned out to be a fraud'.[13]

In a powerful polemical pamphlet for the think-tank the Centre for Policy Studies, Peter Oborne made some serious allegations about Tony Blair's conduct concerning the 'War on Terror'. Oborne, admittedly a right-wing commentator with a low opinion of Blair, maintained the British public were fed 'half-truths, falsehoods and lies'. For Oborne, Blair set out to 'politicise terror' and use it for party-political advantage; he had consistently failed to tell the truth and betrayed the public's trust, contributing to a decline in public confidence in the institutions of government. If true, these assertions constitute a damning indictment of a Prime Minister.[14] Other sources, and not the usual suspects, have chipped in with negative comments. Alastair Campbell's former deputy Lance Price (an ex-BBC reporter) accused Blair of 'rather relishing' his role as a war leader.[15] The BBC has also been accused of a loss of nerve following Hutton, to the extent of downplaying stories critical of the government, including the forced ejection of veteran party member Walter Wolfgang from the Labour Party's 2005 Brighton conference.[16]

The turmoil in Iraq remains to mock Bush and Blair's belief that they possess the power to impose their beliefs on other cultures. The repercussions of Blair's actions for mainland Britain were to be horrendous. In July 2005, Islamic terror came to London. If the London bombs had come before the general election, they might have had more influence on the result; the government's attempts to deny a link between the bombings and the continued occupation of Iraq failed to convince.

Part Three

THE LEGACY

Chapter 11: 2005 and Beyond; an Assessment

Eight years into his premiership, Tony Blair's wish to reconcile the British people to Europe was no nearer fulfilment. By the spring of 2003, Gordon Brown and the Treasury had decided that the five tests for joining the Euro had not been satisfied and crucially, the Euro-zone economies were not matching the UK's growth. Polls were showing increasing public opposition to the Euro, an omen that Blair would not dare to ignore, and the promised referendum on joining the Euro failed to materialise. In the weeks before the 2005 election, Blair told Sky News that while the political case might be strong the economic tests hadn't been met and that 'at the moment' it was unlikely that a referendum would be held during the next parliament.[1] Labour produced another pledge card for the 2005 election campaign. The card contained five vague statements – 'Your family better off: Your child achieving more: Your children with the best start: Your community safer: Your country's borders protected'.[2] Their manifesto went into more detail, including commitments to improving the minimum wage, more parental choice in education, a commitment to an NHS free at the point of delivery, strong action on graffiti, gangs and drug-dealers, the introduction of identity cards and measures to combat bogus asylum seekers and illegal immigration. All in all, the manifesto was the by now familiar mixture of populist authoritarianism and half-hearted welfarism.

Tony Blair won his historic third victory, yet it was not the ringing endorsement he'd wanted from the electorate. Despite facing a Conservative Party whose leader Michael Howard retained an unpleasant whiff of 'something of the night', New Labour's percentage of the vote fell to just 36 per cent and their majority in the Commons was reduced to 66. It was still a very healthy working majority. While there was electoral disquiet about Iraq, the Conservative alternative appeared unpalatable compared to a government that appeared economically competent and was delivering relative stability at home.

> 'Your family better off:
> Your child achieving more:
> Your children with the best start:
> Your community safer:
> Your country's borders protected.'
> Labour Party pledge card 2005

As previously noted, Blair's announcement that he intended to serve a full third term but would not be leading New Labour in a fourth general election campaign was a tactical mistake. Stating publicly that he would go before the general election of 2009 or 2010 was an attempt to appease Gordon Brown and heal the rift between the two most important New Labour politicians that has been a bizarre feature of his government since day one. But it helped create the perception of a lame duck leader. Adding to the idea that Blair was entering his final days, his constituency agent John Burton, not a man who would say anything Blair did not want him to, announced in the summer of 2005 that Tony had told him he did not intend to stand again as an MP once he left Number 10.[3] Leaks at the beginning of 2006 that he would not serve a full term but was planning to give his successor two years to bed himself in as Prime Minister before an election may have been designed to further cement Brown into the Blairite project. If he does take over as leader, Brown will not want to inherit a divided party; with Brown more onside Tony Blair would be able to gain support for policies he hopes will leave a legacy. Shortly after the 2005 election, Blair promised there would be a *stable and orderly transition* but as the uncertainty about his departure time continued and the Brownites discontent became increasingly public, the demands for a timetable mounted.[4]

This is not the place to examine each nook and cranny of Blair's policy agenda and assess his progress in meeting key goals. His success at achieving some of the often vague and rather limited goals his government set, especially in his first term, has been noted earlier. However, a brief summary of his record in some key policy areas suggests what many people feel – 'things can only get better'.

Since 1997, Britain has intervened directly in Iraq (1998) and again in (2003 – ongoing), Kosovo (1999), Sierra Leone (2000), East Timor (2000) and Afghanistan (2001 – ongoing). Robert Cooper, then head of the Cabinet Defence and Overseas Secretariat, described these interventions as 'liberal imperialism'.[5] Some have said this strategy, combined with a Strategic Defence Review that improved the capacity of the armed forces to operate overseas, has enabled Britain to once again become not only a world power, but also 'unquestionably the world's second strongest power'.[6] It has been suggested that when we finally get to see the relevant documents Blair and Bush's relationship could be seen as of similar importance as Churchill and Roosevelt's Second World War partnership.[7] One rather doubts it.

Inevitably, the invasion of Iraq is the issue which has blighted Blair's current reputation. His government lied about the extent of the danger from weapons of mass destruction and appeared determined to attack Iraq whatever the rest of the world thought. The United Nations was dismissed as an irrelevance. The lies led to the repeated use of 'BLIAR' as a placard slogan and Tory election poster. Probably the worst foreign policy decision by a Prime Minister since Eden's over Suez, the invasion has led to more than 100,000 deaths, including (at the time of writing) over 2,000 Coalition soldiers. There was, and is, no clear plan for the re-establishment of order. In many areas of the country, there is effectively civil war and leaks from the British government suggested that, if the insurgency worsened, Coalition forces might have to pull out and leave the competing sides to sort it out themselves. On his return to Iraq in 2006, the BBC's John Simpson found that virtually all the basic services were in a worse state than they were before the invasion and a 'real, abiding anger' in the Iraqi people 'that the richest nation on Earth should have taken over their country and made them even worse off in so many ways than they were before'.[8]

For most people, Iraq will be Blair's chief memorial. Although he has achieved so much more than Anthony Eden, his name will forever be associated with Iraq as Eden's is with Suez. The invasion of Iraq by British forces was a misguided policy that was effectively his alone and tied Britain in with the actions of an American leader who freely admitted God's role in his decision to invade Iraq. On 7 July 2005, during the London rush hour, four suicide bombers killed 52 people and injured many more in attacks on three tube trains and a double-decker bus. Exactly two weeks later, four more suspected bombers failed to ignite their devices in a carbon copy of the first attacks. The identification of the dead bombers as British nationals of Pakistani descent further exacerbated tensions in some communities. Tony Blair played down the connection between the bombings and the invasion and occupation of Iraq, but opinion polls suggested nearly two-thirds of the British people didn't believe him.[9] John Rentoul, a friendly Blair biographer, agreed it was almost certain that the London tube and bus bombings of 2005 were a direct result of Blair's decision to support George Bush's invasion of Iraq.[10] Blair's decision will haunt Britain for some time to come.

One area Blair must expect to be keenly judged on is education, especially given his many statements since 1997 putting it at the top of his reform agenda. In higher education, his policies arouse considerable opposition. Without warning, immediately on entering office for the first time, student grants were abolished; after 2001, top-up fees for university were introduced despite a manifesto commitment that they would not be. At secondary level, exam results have improved, but the improvements have been accompanied by the usual chorus that this is because exams are now easier. Importantly, literacy and numeracy strategies at primary level were an undoubted success. But there appeared to be a lack of coherence to education policy. Muddled thinking abounded; for example, compulsory language classes were announced for primary schools but languages are no longer a compulsory subject for children over 14, a strange decision.

The government's education reform bill proposed a network of self-governing trust schools, giving individual schools more control over their assets and, crucially, their admission policies. Partnerships with local businesses would be encouraged. There was inevitable opposition, and not only from the usual suspects on the left but also from friends and long-term insiders. Fiona Millar described Blair's education reform bill as a 'sort of old right idea, not a new radical progressive idea', and her partner Alastair Campbell's opposition was also suspected. Angela Eagle, a Labour MP from the mainstream of the party, feared that schools outside of local authority control would 'cream off' the most able pupils.[11] Blair was forced to make changes – for example, strengthening the code on admissions to prevent selection by interview and allowing local authorities to open new schools themselves – as he tried to get the bill through Parliament without relying on Tory support.

In 2006, nine years after stressing education was his number one, two and three priority (*sic*), he was struggling to sell a watered-down education reform bill to his own backbenchers. On 15 March 2006, enough Labour MPs rebelled that Blair was faced with a Labour bill only proceeding because of Conservative support, to intense Opposition delight. The pressure upon Deputy Leader John Prescott to support the bill, which Prescott clearly felt uneasy about, suggested this was the area where Blair felt he could make the biggest single impact. But time was running out; as even his long-time supporters like Neil Kinnock began to call for an early departure, his need to secure a legacy became more urgent. To add to Blair's woes on education, the Higher Education Policy Institute announced there was no way, from the current figure of 42.5 per cent, that the government would reach its target of 50 per cent of the population in higher education by 2010.[12]

Blair was determined that Britain's spending on health should at least match the average in the EU and there has been massive extra investment in the NHS. Despite concerns that some of the increases were the result of dodgy accounting procedures, spending has risen by more than 50 per cent in real terms since 1997.[13] However, the increase failed to produce the expected improvements. To be fair, top-down performance management has not been the failure some predicted; many key targets have been met, including reducing waiting times for operations. But meeting those targets has taken large amounts of money. Increases in staff, including 80,000 more doctors and nurses, big pay awards, and a major hospital rebuilding programme, have all impacted on the ability of health trusts to keep to spending targets. In March 2006 the head of the NHS, Sir Nigel Crisp, was effectively forced to resign and take the blame for an accelerating financial crisis. NHS spending will be reined in and future improvements in patient care look difficult to guarantee.[14]

New Labour promised to halve child poverty by 2010 and eliminate it by 2020. Its major strategy to achieve that has appeared to be getting more parents into work. The Child Poverty Action Group say child poverty has declined since Labour came in to power, reversing the upward trend of the 18 years the Conservatives were in government, but the target remains unlikely to be achieved.[15] As with some other policy areas, such as the minimum wage, Labour's impact has not been unfavourable, but it has fallen short of the rhetoric.

The government's lack of commitment to civil liberties has aroused considerable concern and doubt has been expressed about their motives. How did a Shadow Home Secretary committed to civil liberties become, as Prime Minister, a supporter of measures that seriously damage those civil liberties? Identity cards have been an unpopular proposal, yet Tony Blair remains convinced of their potential value. He claimed they would virtually end identity fraud and assist the security forces in the 'War on Terror', even though they had failed to prevent terrorist action in Spain and would have been of no use in preventing the London tube and bus bombings. We were assured they would be voluntary. The disingenuousness of the government showed when it was announced that ID cards would be voluntary but everyone applying for a passport would have their details entered on a national identity register. Effectively, unless one decides never to holiday abroad, ID cards will be compulsory. There were other infringements of civil liberties. The right to a jury trial for some offences was removed. In response to widespread public concern at the failure of the courts to cope with anti-social behaviour by some sections of society, anti-social behaviour orders (Asbos) were introduced on 1 April 1999. Local councils had the power to administer Asbos to juvenile and adult troublemakers accused of anti-social behaviour and then fine or imprison those who broke the terms of the order. The then Home Secretary, Jack Straw, sparked controversy in 2001 when he proposed keeping all fingerprints and DNA samples even if a suspect was acquitted or never charged. Despite protest from civil liberties groups, the Court of Appeal ruled that police could keep DNA and fingerprints from people charged but not convicted, and the Criminal Justice Bill 2005 enshrined this change.[16]

Britain's involvement or compliance with the torture administered in Iraq, Afghanistan and Guantanamo Bay, and the 'extraordinary rendition' flights in which the CIA transported terrorist suspects through British airports to deliver them for torture to places such as Jordan, Afghanistan and Saudi Arabia where human rights are rudimentary at best, shamed our country. Alistair Darling admitted in March 2006 that 73 such extraordinary renditions had occurred since 2001. When David Blunkett became Home Secretary in 2001 the gradual movement towards an authoritarian agenda accelerated. Like many former authoritarian socialists his authoritarian instincts appear to have been deeper than his socialist ones. But what must be remembered is that Blunkett could only do what his master wanted him to do; much of the abuse heaped upon Blunkett's head rightly belongs to Tony Blair.

The potential of other measures to infringe long-held

freedoms caused widespread concern. As noted in Chapter 5, the government's constitutional reform programme has failed to deliver a coherent package of measures. Many changes have strengthened the government's hold on the legislative process. In 2006, the government proposed a Legislative and Regulatory Reform Bill, an effectively permanent constitutional change that would allow ministers to introduce legislation without reference to Parliament: its impact would be far-reaching. For example, the bill could be used to extend parliamentary terms or increase the amount of time a suspect is held without charge. Ministerial fiat, indeed, although a supine House of Commons' failure to act in any way as an independent scrutiniser of government during the Blair years arguably means such a bill is barely necessary. Less cynically, it provides a further example of the essentially authoritarian nature of Tony Blair's government.

Progress on environmental issues has been stymied by a combination of US intransigence and British government incompetence. In the lead-up to the Iraq war, when Bush really needed Blair, more pressure could have been put on the US to sign the Kyoto Agreement which would have tied the major industrial nations into reducing emissions of greenhouse gases. Perhaps something positive might then have come out of that illegal and unnecessary war. Friends of the Earth and Greenpeace have both been critical of New Labour's environmental polices and CO_2 emissions are rising under Blair.[17] The government's review of its programme, delivered in March 2006, was forced to admit that while it was sticking to its target of reducing carbon emissions to 20 per cent below 1990 limits by 2010, it had no idea how this would be achieved. Friends of the Earth called the government's performance 'pathetic'.[18] We are also no nearer a coherent transport policy for the UK than we were in 1997. Seldon calls the government's record an 'embarrassing failure'.[19]

As Tony Blair's time in office neared its end, the desperation emanating from Number 10 was palpable. The process appeared to be, throw it at the wall and see if it sticks. Public service reform was now to be Blair's legacy. And the importance of reform was presented in apocalyptic terms. Unless his reforms were instituted it would be the end of the welfare state, we were warned, although not directly. Policy advisers like Professor Julian le Grand of the London School of Economics were wheeled out to stress the importance of Blair's reforms. For le Grand, Blair's commitment to choice and competition in public services would make them more responsive and efficient and 'contrary to popular belief', more equitable and socially just. Le Grand, a distinguished academic and long-term advocate of what he called 'quasi-markets' in public services – effectively, public and private providers of services competing to deliver the best services and attract 'customers' to state funded but often privately delivered services – argued that unless the public services were redesigned the pressure would be on to cut taxes and Britain would move towards privatisation. In short, the reforms were essential if the Welfare State was to survive.[20] A cynic might argue that it is rather late in Blair's prime ministerial day to be making such essential changes. Early in 2006 on BBC's *Breakfast Time* it was put to Blair that he seemed to have his foot on the accelerator with regard to a raft of reforms and that it all smacked of a man 'who knows he won't be in office much longer'. Blair's response was to laugh and say that big changes had already been made.[21]

Tony Blair's influence could still make a key difference in some areas. Against all expectations, London beat Paris in the contest to hold the 2012 Olympic Games. Blair's contribution in supporting the British team's representations personally was said to have been a crucial factor in changing the minds of some International Olympic Committee delegates. But by spring 2006 there was an undeniable air of *fin de siècle* around his administration. Not only that, the stench of sleaze was beginning to intensify. It would be stretching it to suggest that his or his ministers' actions approached the culture of personal financial corruption that blighted John Major's government. But the rules of political donations were stretched to the limits and despite the denials there were quite clearly knighthoods and peerages being awarded for donations or loans. As more revelations of secret loans in return for honours emerged, the first cartoons personally associating Blair with sleaze began to appear.[22] His was not the first administration to reward supporters with honours, and despite current breast-beating it won't be the last, but Blair had promised a government that would be whiter than white. He had, said Michael Portillo, promised cleaner politics but made them dirtier. The irony of a member of the previous Conservative government, itself sunk by sleaze, putting the boot in, will not have been lost on Blair. Portillo called Blair's plight 'pitiable' as he sank into a 'quagmire of self-manufactured sleaze' and mischievously proposed that, like Captain Boycott before him, Blair's actions had provided us with a handy new noun: 'Blairism' would, in future, be the word whenever 'hypocrisy' seemed too tame.[23] A government that had lived by 'spin' now found itself unable to control the media agenda.

Chapter 12: His Place in History?

In terms of winning elections, Tony Blair is the most successful leader in Labour's history. With an unprecedented three election victories, he will undoubtedly be reckoned a considerable politician. But will he be judged a great man? As Andrew Rawnsley noted, he will be judged not by the size of his majorities but by what he did with them.[1] In 1997 he declared that he would lead *one of the great, radical reforming governments of our history*.[2] Given his desire to leave a legacy which will establish him as a great man, it is remarkable how little has been achieved by this 'extraordinarily feline politician'.[3]

Tony Blair promised that the 'benefits' of Thatcherism would be retained but that the needs of those forgotten or marginalised by her policies would be met. His general message was brilliantly encapsulated in one of New Labour's most famous soundbites, when he promised his government would be *tough on crime* but also *tough on the causes of crime*.

Tony Blair did more than tick all the right boxes. As polls show, people believed he meant what he said; in unprecedented numbers the public <u>trusted</u> him to deliver and help to re-establish their faith in public figures and the democratic process. At the centre of his attraction were a youthfulness, charisma and broad popular appeal previously unknown in British centre-left politics. Perhaps only David Owen of modern politicians, during the brief flowering of the Social

Democrat Party, had similarly captured the popular imagination, but there always appeared something smug and manufactured about Owen. Blair genuinely appeared the *regular sort of guy* he claimed to be and it is easy to forget, with what we now know, how different and exciting he then appeared.

Perhaps too much was riding on him. Perhaps it is unrealistic to expect that after so long in government he could possibly have the same lustre. But there is little doubt that many people feel let down by the retreat from those early commitments. A man who promises high standards of honest and open government, and then re-appoints (and re-appoints!) to high office those like Peter Mandelson and David Blunkett who have flagrantly transgressed those standards, can have few causes for complaint if trust is lost. Just as importantly, if you appeal for trust and are then at the very least disingenuous about the evidence that took Britain to war in Iraq and put the country in the frontline of a world-wide ideological battle, you must expect to find that some people feel betrayed.

Damningly, during Blair's watch there has been a considerable erosion of public trust in politicians. The public's cynicism about the motives of politicians is reaching potentially dangerous levels. Blair had the chance to reverse that trend. Instead, he has confirmed the electorate's worse fears about politicians – they're all the same. The news in March 2006 that Alan B'Stard, the sleazy Conservative MP of the 1980s television series *The New Statesman*, was to be reborn as a corrupt New Labour MP, seemed to capture the zeitgeist of Blair's final years in office.[4]

His promise to restore the public's trust in government looks hollow. Criticism has come from all corners. In August 2005, Sir Alistair Graham, chairman of the Committee on Standards in Public Life, accused the government of being over-concerned with 'control freakery', marginalising ethical standards and failing to protect the Civil Service's impartiality. Crucially, he believed the government's actions over the Iraq war had been a catalyst in diminishing levels of trust.[5] The revelations that emerged of secret loans for honours further scarred Blair's reputation.

Despite the false claims that took Britain to war in Iraq, if there is one single factor that has contributed most to Blair's decline in trust it may be his government's obsession with spin. Mandelson's desire to spin was understandable, given the kicking that the British press gave Neil Kinnock, but the extent to which the Number 10 machinery attempted to bully the print and broadcast news media inevitably had negative effects. The battle to control the news agenda, shown by the creation of rapid rebuttal technology in opposition and unrelenting news management in office, the ruthless treatment of dissenters, and the centralisation of decision-making among a cabal of mostly unelected 'cronies', demonstrates Tony Blair's determination to be synonymous with 'the government'. In hindsight, Margaret Thatcher's Cabinets, their members often dismissed as 'vegetables', contained more debate and deeper ideological divisions than Blair's. Blair has stamped the apparatus of government with his individual personality more than any other British peacetime leader. Blair is New Labour and without him New Labour as we know it would not exist. Therefore, Blair must, to a greater degree than any previous premier, take the full responsibility for his government's record.

The extent of his potential legislative power is demonstrated by his government's extraordinary record in the House of Commons. Their first defeat was on the Terrorism Bill in November 2005, over eight years into office, although two votes on the Racial and Religious Hatred Bill have been lost since then. Strangely, Tony Blair was responsible for one of those later losses, voting in the first division but not in the second, which was lost by one vote; allegedly, he was watching a football match on television. Given this control, it is remarkable how little radical change has been achieved. Of course, his government's lack of personnel with managerial expertise and experience was probably a crucial factor. It is also questionable that Blair, despite his pledge to lead a reforming government, truly sought radical change. More than one critic has seen Blair's role as consolidating the changes Thatcherism introduced. For Professor David Starkey: 'in all important decisions, Blair follows Mrs Thatcher – she's his goal, his idol, his target, his example'.[6]

'In all important decisions, Blair follows Mrs Thatcher – she's his goal, his idol, his target, his example.'

DAVID STARKEY

Both his debt to Thatcher and his religious conviction are alluded to in the title he gave to an opinion piece for *The Daily Telegraph* in 1996 – 'How I Will Follow Her'. The reputation of Thatcher was firmly established by her (*sic*) success in winning the Falklands War. Tony Blair's desire to follow her, in this scenario, may even have influenced his decision to take Britain to war in Iraq.

Margaret Thatcher was constrained by fierce opposition to her policies, not only in the country as a whole but also within her early Cabinets. She was essentially forced to include in her first Cabinets men with whom she disagreed personally and ideologically. Nearly every new policy she introduced was opposed, often violently, in both her party and the country. In contrast, and helped considerably by the battles fought by Thatcher, and by Neil Kinnock within the Labour Party, Blair had unprecedented <u>potential</u> control of the policy-making process. That control was extended into the country by his packing of regional boards and quangos with his own appointments. This could be seen as a necessary procedure to correct 18 years of Conservative appointments, although one such appointee told me that it was made clear to him that if he accepted the appointment his function would be to make sure Tony's wishes were carried out. There is no room for disagreement in Blair's world. The guiding principle is that if you are not 100 per cent for us, you are against us, and Blair's life is littered with the corpses of those who forgot or failed to understand this essential rule.

What drives Tony Blair – what is he in politics for? The man himself has no doubt. A commitment to social justice and a desire to create a fairer, more meritocratic society are at the centre of his political convictions. But like the 'Third Way', an ideology most notable for its lack of clarity about specific courses of action, his statements are vague and fail to pass an important test – how could one argue for a 'less fair' society for example? In his 1996 'vision' for the country, he put forward four *cornerstones* for the new Britain he sought to create. He would improve standards of living, create *a true community of citizens*, deliver accountability and decentralisation for political institutions to *put the people in power*, and deliver *leadership and confidence* in Europe and beyond.[7] In none of these areas could even his staunchest supporter claim he has had significant success and arguably he has failed to deliver any of them.

It is undeniable that there is a sense of an opportunity lost. Blair himself has expressed regret that he has not been bolder. New Labour's majorities have given it a powerful electoral mandate for change; the last time a Labour government was given such a mandate was 1945 and the social change achieved by that government – led by a far less charismatic figure – still reverberates today. Will anything Blair's government has done still echo in 50 or more years' time? The question is less inconsequential than it might appear. Like many leaders approaching the end of their time, Blair appears

Tony Blair's legacy

Foreign Policy: For many, Iraq will be Blair's chief legacy. The invasion of Iraq was a misguided policy that was effectively his alone and tied Britain in with the US. Britain is now a key terrorist target.

Education: In higher education, student grants were abolished, and top-up fees for university were introduced. At secondary level, exam results have consistently improved. Importantly, literacy and numeracy strategies at primary level are an undoubted success.

Health and welfare: NHS spending has risen by more than 50 per cent in real terms since 1997 but increases in staff and a hospital rebuilding programme have created a financial crisis. For now, NHS spending will be reined in and future improvements in patient care look unlikely. Child poverty has declined but Blair's aim to halve child poverty by 2010 looks unlikely to be achieved.

Civil liberties: Blair's legacy is a more authoritarian state. ID cards will soon be (effectively) compulsory. Anti-social behaviour orders instituted the possibility of imprisonment without trial. The Criminal Justice Bill 2005 allows police to keep DNA and fingerprints from people charged but not convicted.

Constitutional reform: Blair declared that he would lead 'one of the great, radical reforming governments of our history'. His government has failed to deliver coherent constitutional reform; many changes have strengthened the government's hold on the legislative process.

Environment and transport: CO_2 emissions are rising and Blair's government has admitted it has no idea how to achieve its target of reducing carbon emissions. In transport, we are no nearer a coherent policy for the UK than we were in 1997.

The economy: A success – but is it Brown's legacy rather than Blair's? Despite record levels of personal debt and mortgage repossessions, Britain has experienced one of its longest periods of economic stability. The introduction of the minimum wage deserves credit.

Blair raised hopes of great achievement but generally failed to deliver. During his watch, there has been a considerable erosion of public trust in politicians. Perhaps history will see Blair's legacy as consolidating Thatcherism.

increasingly obsessed by his historical legacy. Blair has had, like Margaret Thatcher, plenty of luck throughout his career. The difference is that Thatcher took advantage of her luck to fundamentally shift society in the direction she wished. Blair has ridden his luck rather than used it to achieve the things he claims he wants. The vague goals that he hoped would provide his legacy were enunciated and initiated too late in his premiership, requiring a degree of administrative co-ordination that increasingly appeared beyond Tony Blair's ability. All that charisma, all that potential, all that power, has been largely misspent.

The problem for the Blair government was that in opposition they had been so careful not to give any hostages to fortune that they failed to develop a coherent, let alone radical, policy programme. Once in office, nothing was allowed to thwart a potentially historic second victory. His desire to achieve his policy agenda in his second term was frustrated by the demands of a national foot and mouth crisis that straddled the election and by the attacks on the World Trade Center. As he struggled to put together a legacy in his third term he was saddled with the lame duck perception. It appears his opportunity to leave a significant footprint has been missed.

Talking in 2001, Bryan Gould said he didn't think Blair was a politician at all because while he had principles and courage, he lacked a 'serious analysis of society and what must be improved'.[8] It is apparent that Blair's inability to develop a clear policy programme across the range of governmental responsibilities is a contributory factor in his failure to leave a coherent and significant legacy. For others, his limited understanding of the machinery of government and his lack of understanding of the need to get the systems right before effective change can be made, combined with his impatience at the processes by which change must be managed, have been crucial factors.[9] As already noted, the paucity of managerial experience in both Blair and his appointments has been a serious weakness.

His failure to develop a harmonious relationship with the second most important politician in his inner circle must also be a consideration. What might have been achieved with Gordon Brown onside? Brown and Blair were a partnership to rival any in political history before Brown's resentment at not succeeding John Smith became something that soured him. From 1994, the relationship was one of increasing bitterness, with a 'steady seepage of bile and contempt' towards the Prime Minister and his acolytes. Better man-management was needed and Blair's mishandling of his Chancellor has been one of his major mistakes.[10] Blair's greater commitment to market solutions was bound to create some problems but there should have been more effort to repair the schism at the heart of government.

While Brown effectively operated alone in managing the economy, there was an extraordinary concentration of decision making within the Prime Minister's small office. Blair was uncomfortable with intellectuals and Alastair Campbell despised them so there was little 'intellectual' input into the consideration of policy alternatives. His close core of insiders were the driving forces of policy. 'Results, not procedures' – outputs not ideology – became a defining characteristic of New Labour. Cabinet government was rendered non-existent; advice from ministers was rarely sought and serious Cabinet discussions became even rarer. Some of Blair's ministerial appointments were, in Clement Attlee's famous condemnation, 'not up to it'; poor Estelle Morris clearly suffered during her brief time as Education Secretary. The relative lack of formal decision-making procedures generated criticism from the top civil servants especially. His over-reliance on focus groups also meant that his government appeared to lack leadership and was essentially reactive.

Inevitably, any assessment of the man and his government's record will be subjective; Blairites will have a positive perspective on his record while his many critics will paint a more negative picture. Quite clearly, his premiership has not been a 'failure'. Indeed, if you believe that 'it's the economy, stupid', his government's record has been incredibly successful. Although Britain has record levels of personal debt and mortgage repossessions, we have experienced one of the longest periods of economic stability in our history; Gordon Brown's management of the economy has given New Labour a reputation for financial probity. While there are record lows in public trust in politicians, there is no widespread feeling that this is an incompetent government. Some things are better now, some are worse than in 1997. Blair's governance of this country has by no means been wholly unsuccessful, and he must be given credit for at least keeping the ship steady. All in all, and while admitting that much of this is down to 'luck' in the form of a stable world economy and a lack of deep fissures in society, we live in a country where most things function fairly well. It could be worse. But it could have been so much better.

Parts of Blair's personal agenda, developed in opposition and in power, were extremely ambitious. His agenda included wishing to make a key contribution to ending the Arab-Israeli conflict, eliminating child poverty in Britain, putting half of the population through university, changing the way the people of Britain regard the European Union and ending both AIDS and poverty in Africa. It is no surprise that progress (if any) towards those goals has been slow. History may one day recognise his contribution towards such noble aims. Perhaps, also, in a few years time we may look back upon his decade in office as a time of unprecedented economic stability and prosperity. Who knows, we may talk of the 'Blair years' with the same sort of warm and cosy affection with which people of a certain age look back upon Dennis Compton, Spangles, Alma Cogan and Radio Luxembourg. For the moment, that appears unlikely. But who knows?

As his time in office ebbs away Blair has become obsessed with his legacy. A whole raft of reforms, many already compromised by his failure to persuade his own party of their merit, are being spun as leaving a 'legacy any prime minister could and should be proud of'[12] but for many he has left it too late. As Max Hastings has waspishly remarked, it is amazing that such an intelligent man believes he can, among other things, reform public services, reconcile the British people to his European vision and leave a stable government in Iraq in the short time before he leaves.[13] Even if the objectives are attainable, which is improbable, it is unlikely that he would be remembered for them.

Beckett and Hencke have ridiculed attempts to portray Blair as the direct successor to Clement Attlee's reforming post-war Labour government. For them, Attlee's government made 'staggering' improvements to the lives of ordinary British people while Blair has widened the gap between rich and poor. While acknowledging that Blair has been rather more successful, they believe the appropriate comparison is with Ramsey MacDonald, Prime Minister for the first two years of the National Government of 1929. Both were vain and theatrical, both deferred to the rich and titled, both accepted holidays in the homes of the wealthy, both disliked the traditional ideology of the Labour Party and both shared a desire to forge a national consensus above politics.[14]

I would argue that a more appropriate analogy is with Harold Wilson, another Labour leader who entered office with high public expectations. Both had assumed leadership unexpectedly, each replacing a popular leader who had died suddenly. Both won their first election as leader and came into government replacing a long-term Conservative government racked by scandal; both men seemed young and squeaky-clean by comparison. Both sought to present themselves as the 'people's prime minister'; Wilson, an Oxford don, cultivated a Yorkshire accent, while Blair attempted to adopt the increasingly universal sound of estuary English when addressing the nation. Both cultivated showbiz connections and posed with the latest pop stars; Wilson with The Beatles and Blair with Noel Gallagher of the heavily Beatles-influenced Oasis were equally aware of the publicity value of such associations. Despite Blair's admission of technological ignorance concerning his iPod, both men embodied modernity and the 'white heat of the technological revolution'. Both cultivated an inner cabinet of unelected advisers. Finally, both Wilson and Blair came into office with the promise of great things and Blair, like Wilson, appears increasingly likely to be leaving with that promise unfulfilled. Chillingly for Blair, Wilson's resignation was accompanied by the allegations of sleaze and cash for honours that now accompany Blair in his political dotage. It appears that when Blair does finally go it will be, like Wilson, without trumpets or honour.

History will consign to its footnotes some 20th-century Prime Ministers who might have aspired to greatness but ended up drifting through their premiership such as Stanley Baldwin and John Major. Of Blair's post-war predecessors, perhaps only three will be senior figures in British history. As a great wartime leader and the embodiment of certain national characteristics, Winston Churchill reigns supreme, regularly voted the greatest Briton to the bemusement of those championing William Shakespeare. The scale and essential permanence of the 1945 Labour government's creation of the welfare state has long been clear, but only recently have Clement Attlee's leadership and managerial qualities begun to be properly appreciated.[15] Attlee's place in history is secure and his reputation is growing. For different reasons, Margaret Thatcher's achievements ensure her a place in the pantheon of 'great' men and women. Thatcher may be an unpopular choice with some critics but the scale of her achievements in the face of huge opposition (whatever one may think of those achievements) and the cult of personality that surrounded her, means she leaves a giant footprint. At the moment, Tony Blair appears unlikely to join these three heavyweights.

Blair sought a place among the elite of great modern British leaders. He could have had the place on the empty plinth in Trafalgar Square, surrounded by Attlee, Churchill and Thatcher. His place in history is assured, but it's not the place he would have sought. The plinth was waiting for him. In 1997, Blair could have achieved anything but his premiership petered out in a series of half-baked reforms, sleaze and spin. Tony Blair's inability or unwillingness to understand that the British people were willing him to be different, to genuinely be *a pretty straight sort of guy* rather than yet another disingenuous and weasel-mouthed politician, has destroyed his chances of being remembered in the way he wished. For Thatcher, office was the means to an end. For Blair, getting and holding on to office became more important than doing something with that office. He *will* go down in history as a big name, but for the wrong reasons, held up as history's warning to the faint-hearted. He who dares, wins. Historians will cite him as the man who was scared to dare; a prime minister who raised hopes of great achievement, who had the majority and the public backing to deliver a new kind of politics for a new century, but who failed to deliver.

NOTES

Introduction

1. Francis Beckett and David Hencke, *The Survivor: Tony Blair in peace and war* (Aurum Press, London: 2005) p viii, hereafter Beckett and Hencke (2005).

Chapter 1: Tony Blair's Childhood

1. John Rentoul, *Tony Blair, Prime Minister* (Warner Books, London: 2001) p 6, hereafter Rentoul (2001).
2. Jon Sopel, *Tony Blair the Moderniser* (Bantam Books, London: 1995) p 8, hereafter Sopel (1995).
3. Beckett and Hencke (2005), p 4.
4. Sopel (1995), p 9.
5. Sopel (1995), in Leo Abse, *The Man Behind the Smile: Tony Blair and the politics of perversion* (London, Robson Books: 1996), pp 113–14, hereafter Abse (1996).
6. Abse (1996), p 114.
7. David Kennedy cited in Rentoul (2001), p 21.
8. Rentoul (2001).
9. Beckett and Hencke (2005), p 6.
10. Anthony Seldon, *Blair* (Free Press, London: 2005) p 5, hereafter Seldon (2005).
11. Beckett and Hencke (2005), p 6.
12. Seldon (2005), p 7; Beckett and Hencke (2005), p 7.
13. Beckett and Hencke (2005), p 13
14. In Ed Black, 'Tony Blair's revolting schooldays', *The Scotsman*, 23 July 2004.
15. Seldon (2005), p 233.
16. Seldon (2005), p 235.

17. Beckett and Hencke (2005), p 18.
18. Seldon (2005), p 11.

Chapter 2: Oxford, the Bar and Cherie
1. *Tony Blair Rock Star*, Channel 4, 19 January 2006.
2. Seldon (2005), p 27.
3. *Tony Blair Rock Star* (2006).
4. Rentoul (2001), p 132.
5. Abse (1996), p 131.
6. Seldon (2005), pp 39–45.
7. Rentoul (2001), p 3.
8. Seldon (2005), p 36.
9. Rentoul (2001), p 225; Seldon (2005), p 70.
10. Beckett and Hencke (2005), p 269

Chapter 3: Tony Blair, Fledgling Politician
1. Keith Proud, *Grit in the Oyster: the biography of John Burton* (*The Northern Echo*, Darlington: 2003), pp 100–21, hereafter Proud (2003).
2. Proud (2003), p 121.
3. Seldon (2005), p 99.

Chapter 4: The Road to the Leadership
1. Andrew Rawnsley, *Servants of the People: The inside story of New Labour* (Penguin, London: 2001) pp 315–6, hereafter Rawnsley (2001).
2. Beckett and Hencke (2005), pp 139–61.
3. Al-jazeera.com, 'Tony Blair', 1 January 2003.
4. Tom Bower, *Gordon Brown* (Harper Perennial, London: 2005) p 144, hereafter Bower (2005).
5. Derek Scott, *Off Whitehall* (I B Taurus, London: 2004).
6. Seldon (2005), p 134.
7. Rawnsley (2001), pp 192–9.

8. Dominic Lawson, 'Some taxing questions for Cameron', *The Independent,* 31 January 2006.
9. Michael Temple, 'New Labour's Third Way: pragmatism and governance', *British Journal of Politics and International Relations*, Vol. 2 (3) (2000), hereafter Temple (2000).

Chapter 5: Blair's First Term: an Opportunity Lost

1. Cited in *The Independent*, 15 June 2004.
2. BBC News Online, 21 November 2002.
3. Seldon (2005), p 286.
4. Seldon (2005), p 343.
5. Rawnsley (2001), pp 97–8.
6. *Electronic Telegraph*, No. 910, 20 November 1997.
7. BBC1, *On the Record*, 16 November 1997.
8. Rawnsley (2001), pp 219–26.
9. Bower, *Gordon Brown*, p 291.
10. Geoffrey Robinson, *An Unconventional Minister: My life inside New Labour* (Michael Joseph, London: 2000), hereafter Robinson (2000).
11. Rawnsley (2001), pp 57–8.
12. 'Bagehot', 'Blair's Ceausescu moment', *The Economist*, 16 June 2000, pp 45–8.
13. Rawnsley (2001), p 377.

Chapter 6: In the Court of King Anthony

1. Seldon (2005), p 696.
2. Seldon (2005), p 688.
3. Temple (2000), p 304.
4. Seldon (2005), pp 175–6.
5. Peter Oborne, *Alastair Campbell* (Aurum Press London: 1999) p 108.
6. Seldon (2005), p 294.

7. Beckett and Hencke (2005), p 263.
8. Peter Oborne and Simon Walters, *Alastair Campbell* (Aurum Press, London: 2004).
9. Seldon (2005), p 692.
10. Will Hutton, 'All the president's men and women', *The Guardian*, 24 October 1999, hereafter Hutton (1999).
11. Seldon (2005), pp 309–10.
12. Charlie Whelan, 'He's in the pink, and staying that way', *The Independent Media Weekly*, 27 February 2006.
13. Seldon (2005), p 301.
14. Beckett and Hencke (2005), p 90.
15. Beckett and Hencke (2005), pp 262–82.
16. Beckett and Hencke (2005), pp 102, 156.
17. Seldon (2005), p 136.
18. BBC Radio 4, *Look Back at Power*, 5 September 2005.
19. Hutton (1999).
20. Seldon (2005), pp 345–6
21. Jackie Ashley, 'Quiet rise of the King of Downing Street', *The Guardian,* 14 July 2004.
22. Beckett and Hencke (2005), p 274.
23. *The Scotsman*, 26 May 2003.
24. Hutton (1999).
25. Seldon (2005), p 201.
26. Seldon (2005), p 554.
27. Beckett and Hencke (2005), p 354.
28. BBC News Online, 14 July 2004.
29. Hutton (1999); Steve Richards 'The truth about Downing Street', *The Independent*, 2 September 2005.
30. BBC Radio 4, *Look Back at Power*, 5 September 2005.

Chapter 7: 'Gordon and Tony were lovers …'

1. Tim Shipman 'Relations at a new low as Brown "plots" to oust Blair', *Daily Mail,* 1 April 2006.

2. Bower (2005), pp 77–8.

3. Seldon (2005), p 659.

4. Rentoul (2001), p 128.

5. Paul Routledge, *Gordon Brown: the biography* (Simon & Schuster, London: 1998), pp 204–5; Bower (2005), pp 128–30.

6. Seldon (2005), p 657–89.

7. Paul Routledge, *Gordon Brown*

8. Paul Routledge, *Mandy: the unauthorised biography of Peter Mandelson* (Simon & Schuster, London: 1999).

9. Bill Hagerty, 'Cap'n Spin does lose his rag', *British Journalism Review*, Vol 11 (2) (2000) p 15.

10. Rawnsley (2001), pp 210–11.

11. Scott, *Off Whitehall*, 2004.

12. David Cracknell and David Smith, 'No. 10 aide blows lid on Blair-Brown feud' *The Sunday Times*, 12 September 2004.

13. Robert Peston, *Brown's Britain* (Short Books, London: 2004).

14. Bower (2005), pp 474–5

15. Geoff Mulgan, cited in BBC Radio 4, *Look Back at Power*, 5 September 2005.

16. Robinson (2000), p 185.

17. Bower (2005), p 283.

18. David Rowan, 'Profile: Gavyn Davies', *Evening Standard*, 19 September 2001.

19. Bower (2005), p 327.

20. *The Guardian*, 10 January 2005.

21. Bower (2005), pp 475–6.

22. Bower (2005), p 458.

23. Bower (2005), p 440.

24. ICM poll, *News of the World*, 2 April 2006.

Chapter 8: International Statesman

1. Eytan Gilbao, 'The CNN effect: the search for a communication theory of international relations', *Political Communication,* Vol. 22 (2005), pp 27–44.
2. Rawnsley (2001), p 282.
3. Rawnsley (2001), p 288.
4. Rawnsley (2001), p 290.
5. Seldon (2005), p 407.
6. Rawnsley (2001), p 281.
7. BBC's Analysis and Research Department, 3 May 2002.
8. John Turner 'The policy process' in B Axford *et al* (eds), *Politics: An introduction* (Routledge, London: 2002) pp 445–9.
9. ABC Australia, 26 March 2006.

Chapter 9: Religion and Family

1. Peter Stothard, *Thirty Days: A month at the heart of Blair's war* (Harper Collins, London: 2003) p 191.
2. ITV1, *Parkinson*, 4 March 2006.
3. ITV1, *Parkinson*, 4 March 2006.
4. BBC News Online, 3 May 2003.
5. Beckett and Hencke (2005), p 44.
6. *Daily Telegraph*, 4 May 2003.
7. Labour Party political broadcast, April 1997.
8. ITV1, *Parkinson*, 4 March 2006.
9. Seldon (2005), p 243.
10. BBC News Online, 6 July 2000.
11. Beckett and Hencke (2005), pp 256–7.
12. Jackie Storer, 'Blair's family life under spotlight' BBC News Online, 28 March 2006.
13. Seldon (2005), p 547.
14. Beckett and Hencke (2005), pp 276–8.
15. Beckett and Hencke (2005), p 277.

16. ITV1, *Parkinson*, 4 March 2006.
17. *Daily Mail*, 26 October 2005.
18. Seldon (2005), p 628.
19. Beckett and Hencke (2005), p 329.

Chapter 10: Iraq and the War on Terror

1. Beckett and Hencke (2005), p 298.
2. BBC News, 24 September 2002.
3. Beckett and Hencke (2005), pp 298–9.
4. Bob Woodward, *Plan of Attack* (Simon & Schuster, London: 2004) p 25.
5. Matthew d'Ancona, 'Don't mention the war (or the euro) to Mr Blair', *Sunday Telegraph*, 18 August 2002.
6. Beckett and Hencke (2005), p 299.
7. Simon Jenkins, 'Blair's fundamentalism is the real enemy of western values', *Sunday Times*, 26 March 2006.
8. YouGov poll, *Daily Telegraph*, 25 July 2003.
9. The Hutton Report, Chapter 12, 467. 3 (i).
10. Boris Johnson, 'The BBC was doing its job – bring back Gilligan', *Daily Telegraph,* 29 January 2004.
11. In Beckett and Hencke (2005), p 298.
12. Seldon (2005), pp 647–52.
13. Boris Johnson, 'The BBC was doing its job – bring back Gilligan', *Daily Telegraph,* 29 January 2004.
14. Peter Oborne, *The Use and Abuse of Terror: the construction of a false narrative on the domestic terror threat* (Centre for Policy Studies, London: 2006).
15. *The Mail on Sunday*, 18 September 2005.
16. John Kampfner, 'A very corporate loss of nerve', *New Statesman,* 10 September 2005.

Chapter 11: 2005 and Beyond; an Assessment

1. *Sky News*, 27 April 2005.

2. Labour Party pledge card 2005.

3. *The Guardian*, 2 August 2005.

4. *The Independent,* 30 March 2006.

5. James M Rogers and Matthew Jamison, 'British external policy', 1 May 2005, Henry Jackson Society.

6. N Ferguson, *Empire: How Britain Made the Modern World* (Allen Lane, London: 2003), cited in Rogers and Jamison, 'British external policy'.

7. Martin Gilbert quoted in Seldon (2005), p 702.

8. BBC News Online, 20 March 2006.

9. ICM poll, *The Guardian*, 18 July 2005.

10. John Rentoul, *Independent on Sunday*, 10 July 2005.

11. BBC1, *Panorama*, 12 March 2006.

12. BBC Radio 4 *Today*, 21 March 2006.

13. HM Treasury, Public Expenditure Statistical Analyses 2005.

14. Jeremy Laurance, 'How did things go wrong for the NHS?', *The Independent*, 9 March 2006.

15. Andrew Grice 'Government set to miss its target in fight against child poverty', *The Independent*, 9 March 2006.

16. BBC News Online, 28 March 2006.

17. *The Independent*, 22 March 2006.

18. *The Times*, 29 March 2006.

19. Seldon (2005), p 706.

20. Julian le Grand 'The Blair Legacy? Choice and competition in public services', public lecture, London School of Economics, 21 February 2006, hereafter le Grand (2006).

21. In BBC1, *Panorama: Tony Blair's Long Goodbye*, 12 March 2006.

22. For example, Griffin, *The Sun*, 14 March 2006; Gerald Scarfe, *The Sunday Times*, 19 March 2006; Peter Brookes, *The Times*, 22 March 2006.
23. Michael Portillo, 'Brown can run for the top job but he can't hide', *Sunday Times*, 26 March 2006.

Chapter 12: His Place in History?

1. Rawnsley (2001), p 508.
2. Speech to Labour Party Conference, Brighton, 30 September 1997.
3. Seldon (2005), p xiv.
4. *Daily Telegraph*, 21 March 2006.
5. Marie Woolf, 'Blair accused of failing to restore the public's trust in government's, *The Independent*, 31 August 2005.
6. BBC1, *Question Time*, 6 October 2005.
7. Tony Blair, *New Britain: My vision of a young country* (Fourth Estate, London: 1996) pp vii–viii.
8. Bryan Gould, quoted in Joe Klein, 'Tony Blair – true colours', *The Guardian*, 7 June 2001.
9. Max Hastings, 'Sorry, prime minister, your legacy will be a disastrous foreign war', *The Guardian,* 5 December 2005: Seldon (2005), p 694, hereafter Hastings (2005).
10. Seldon (2005), pp 699–704.
11. Seldon (2005), p 696.
12. le Grand (2006).
13. Hastings (2005).
14. Francis Beckett and David Hencke, 'Policy-free past master', *The Guardian*, 29 September 2004.
15. Francis Beckett, *Clem Attlee* (Politico's, London: 2000).

CHRONOLOGY

Year	Premiership

1997   2 May: Tony Blair wins the election and becomes the youngest of the 20th century prime ministers, aged 43 when he assumes office.

Bank of England given freedom to set interest rates.

Northern Ireland peace talks restarted.

Hong Kong handed back to China.

IRA restore ceasefire.

Foreign Secretary Robin Cook leaves his wife.

Diana Princess of Wales killed in car-crash in Paris: Blair coins phrase *the people's princess*.

'Yes' votes for devolved Welsh and Scottish Assemblies.

Donations to Labour Party by Formula One boss Bernie Ecclestone revealed.

1998   Routledge biography of Gordon Brown reveals his resentment of the PM.

Good Friday Agreement in Northern Ireland.

'Yes' votes in referendums for London mayor and assembly, and for Northern Irish assembly.

Minimum wage announced.

Ron Davies resigns as Welsh Secretary.

Operation Desert Fox (aka 'Monica's War'): UK/US air attacks on Iraq.

Peter Mandelson and Geoffrey Robinson resign from government over home loan scandal.

1999   NATO bombing of Yugoslavia begins. Elections for devolved parliaments in Scotland and Wales – Labour does not win a majority in either.

Milosevic agrees terms on Kosovo with NATO.

Mandelson returns to government as Northern Ireland Secretary.

The Blairs announce they are expecting their fourth child.

Elections to Northern Irish assembly.

31 December: Tony Blair attends Millennium celebrations at the Dome at the end of the 20th century.

History	Culture
Kofi Annan replaces Butros Butros Ghali as UN Secretary General.	Orlando Figes, *A People's Tragedy.*
	Ted Hughes, *Tales from Ovid.*
Israel withdraws troops from Hebron.	J K Rowling, *Harry Potter and the Philosopher's Stone.*
In France, Socialist Party wins general election – Lionel Jospin becomes Prime Minister.	Elton John, *Candle in the Wind.*
Fiji rejoins the Commonwealth.	Katrina and the Waves win the Eurovision Song Contest for the United Kingdom.
	Films: *The Full Monty. LA Confidential. Men in Black. Titanic.*
	TV: *Teletubbies.*
European countries agree on the Euro.	Nick Hornby, *About a Boy.*
President Suharto of Indonesia steps down after 32 years in office.	J K Rowling, *Harry Potter and the Chamber of Secrets.*
India and Pakistan conduct series of nuclear tests.	All Saints, *Never Ever.*
Former Chilean dictator Augusto Pinochet arrested in London.	Céline Dion *My Heart Will Go On*
President Clinton denies affair with Monica Lewinsky: Starr report later calls for his impeachment.	Films: *The Blair Witch Project. Elizabeth. Saving Private Ryan.*
	TV: *Who Wants to be a Millionaire?.*
Euro currency introduced.	Anthony Beevor, *Stalingrad.*
Death of King Hussein of Jordan.	J M Coetzee, *Disgrace.*
US President Clinton acquitted in impeachment trial.	Joanne Harris, *Chocolat.*
	Frank McCourt, *'Tis.*
Hungary, Poland and the Czech Republic join NATO.	J K Rowling, *Harry Potter and the Prisoner of Azkaban.*
Australians vote to retain the Queen as Head of State.	Cher, *Believe.*
	Lou Bega, *Mambo No. 5.*
First major anti-globalisation demonstrations at WTO meeting in Seattle.	Films: *The Matrix. The Sixth Sense. Three Kings. Star Wars Episode 1: The Phantom Menace.*
	TV: *Queer as Folk.*

FURTHER READING

There have so far been five significant biographies of Blair and a number of other books which have examined his associates. Some, like Jon Sopel's early biography (Bantam Books, London: 1995), which gives its slant away by its subtitle *the moderniser*, and John Rentoul's well-researched book (Warner Books, London: 2001), are perhaps overly sympathetic to their subject, lacking an essential critical edge; they are also both dated. Andrew Rawnsley's *Servants of the People* (Penguin, London: 2001) is focussed on the first period in government and examines in close detail the inner workings of the Downing Street coterie; it is an excellent and well-informed read, but again, things have moved on since 2001. Leo Abse's entertaining psychological profile of Blair, *The Man Behind the Smile* (Robson Books, London: 1996), appears remarkably prescient in some of its judgements, notably in seeing the essential timidity of Blair's approach, but the book will tell you little reliable about his early life. Philip Stephens' *Tony Blair* (Viking Books, New York: 2004) is well-written and sympathetic, but its assessment of Blair is aimed primarily at an American audience. On Blair's associates. Tom Bower's *Gordon Brown* (Harper Perennial, London: 2005) pulls few punches in its forensic examination and is especially useful on the Brown-Blair relationship

Without doubt, the two best reads on Blair – although for different reasons – are Anthony Seldon's monumental biography *Blair* (updated edition, Free Press, London: 2005) and Francis Beckett and David Hencke's entertaining *The Survivor: Tony Blair in Peace and War* (updated edition, Aurum

Press, London: 2005). Seldon's approach – 20 chronological chapters, interrupted by 20 profiles of the people most influential in Blair's personal and political life – has been criticised, but this reader found it an extraordinarily useful device with which to navigate Blair's life. Throughout, the quality of the writing and insight, as with all Seldon's work, is first class. An essentially sympathetic biography, the book's conclusion, a less than ringing endorsement of Blair's achievements, therefore carries considerable weight. However, for sheer entertainment, Beckett and Hencke's book can't be beaten, although if you are broadly sympathetic to Blair you may be outraged by the book's view of him. Critical and polemical, by turns waspish and weighty in its judgements, and very well-informed by both attribution and gossip, it was written totally without the Prime Minister's co-operation, unlike the other biographies on Blair. He must have suspected their judgement on his premiership would be brutal. Either of these two books would be good places to start a deeper examination of the life and political significance of Tony Blair.

PICTURE SOURCES

Page vi
Before the landslide, Tony Blair addresses a Labour
conference, 23 January 1997.
(Courtesy Topham Picturepoint)

Page 45
On the doorstep of 10 Downing Street, Tony Blair awaits
the arrival of the new German Chancellor Angela Merkel,
24 November 2005. (Courtesy Topham Picturepoint)

Pages 130–1
Tony Blair being interviewed in the Cabinet Room at 10
Downing Street on 9 October 2001.
(Courtesy Topham Picturepoint)

INDEX

THE 20 BRITISH PRIME MINISTERS
OF THE 20TH CENTURY

Salisbury

SALISBURY
Conservative politician, prime minister 1885–6, 1886–92 and 1895–1902, and the last to hold that office in the House of Lords.

by Eric Midwinter
Visiting Professor of Education at Exeter University
ISBN 1-904950-54-X (pb)

Balfour

BALFOUR
Balfour wrote that Britain favoured 'the establishment in Palestine of a national home for the Jewish people', the so-called 'Balfour Declaration'.

by Ewen Green
of Magdalen College Oxford
ISBN 1-904950-55-8 (pb)

Campbell-Bannerman

CAMPBELL-BANNERMAN
Liberal Prime Minister, who started the battle with the Conservative-dominated House of Lords.

by Lord Hattersley
former Deputy Leader of the Labour Party and Cabinet member in Wilson and Callaghan's governments.
ISBN 1-904950-56-6 (pb)

ASQUITH

His administration laid the foundation of Britain's welfare state, but he was plunged into a major power struggle with the House of Lords.

by Stephen Bates
a senior correspondent for the *Guardian*.
ISBN 1-904950-57-4 (pb)

LLOYD GEORGE

By the end of 1916 there was discontent with Asquith's management of the war, and Lloyd George schemed secretly with the Conservatives in the coalition government to take his place.

by Hugh Purcell
television documentary maker.
ISBN 1-904950-58-2 (pb)

BONAR LAW

In 1922 he was the moving spirit in the stormy meeting of Conservative MPs which ended the coalition, created the 1922 Committee and reinstated him as leader.

by Andrew Taylor
Professor of Politics at the University of Sheffield.
ISBN 1-904950-59-0 (pb)

BALDWIN

Baldwin's terms of office included two major political crises, the General Strike and the Abdication.

by Anne Perkins
a journalist, working mostly for the *Guardian*, as well as a historian of the British labour movement.
ISBN 1-904950-60-4 (pb)

MACDONALD

MacDonald

In 1900 he was the first secretary of the newly formed Labour Representation Committee (the original name for the Labour party). Four years later he became the first Labour prime minister.

by Kevin Morgan

who teaches government and politics at Manchester University.

ISBN 1-904950-61-2 (pb)

CHAMBERLAIN

Chamberlain

His name will forever be linked to the policy of appeasement and the Munich agreement he reached with Hitler.

by Graham Macklin

manager of the research service at the National Archives.

ISBN 1-904950-62-0 (pb)

CHURCHILL

Churchill

Perhaps the most determined and inspirational war leader in Britain's history.

by Chris Wrigley

who has written about David Lloyd George, Arthur Henderson and W E Gladstone.

ISBN 1-904950-63-9 (pb)

ATTLEE

Attlee

His post-war government enacted a broad programme of socialist legislation in spite of conditions of austerity. His legacy: the National Health Service.

by David Howell

Professor of Politics at the University of York and an expert in Labour's history.

ISBN 1-904950-64-7 (pb)

EDEN

His premiership will forever be linked to the fateful Suez Crisis.

by Peter Wilby

former editor of the *New Statesman*.

ISBN 1-904950-65-5 (pb)

MACMILLAN

He repaired the rift between the USA and Britain created by Suez and secured for Britain co-operation on issues of nuclear defence, but entry into the EEC was vetoed by de Gaulle in 1963.

by Francis Beckett

author of BEVAN, published by Haus in 2004.

ISBN 1-904950-66-3 (pb)

DOUGLAS-HOME

Conservative politician and prime minister 1963-4, with a complex career between the two Houses of Parliament.

by David Dutton

who teaches History at Liverpool University.

ISBN 1-904950-67-1 (pb)

WILSON

He held out the promise progress, of 'the Britain that is going to be forged in the white heat of this revolution'. The forced devaluation of the pound in 1967 frustrated the fulfilment of his promises.

by Paul Routledge

The *Daily Mirror's* chief political commentator.

ISBN 1-904950-68-X (pb)

Heath

HEATH

A passionate European, he succeeded during his premiership in effecting Britain's entry to the EC.

by Denis MacShane

Minister for Europe in Tony Blair's first government.

ISBN 1-904950-69-8 (pb)

Callaghan

CALLAGHAN

His term in office was dominated by industrial unrest, culminating in the 'Winter of Discontent'.

by Harry Conroy

When James Callaghan was Prime Minister, Conroy was the Labour Party's press officer in Scotland, and he is now editor of the Scottish *Catholic Observer.*

ISBN 1-904950-70-1 (pb)

Thatcher

Major

Blair

THATCHER

Britain's first woman prime minister and the longest serving head of government in the 20th century (1979–90), but also the only one to be removed from office in peacetime by pressure from within her own party.

by Clare Beckett
teaches social policy at Bradford University.

ISBN 1-904950-71-X (pb)

MAJOR

He enjoyed great popularity in his early months as prime minister, as he seemed more caring than his iron predecessor, but by the end of 1992 nothing seemed to go right.

by Robert Taylor
is Research Associate at the LSE's Centre for Economic Performance.
ISBN 1-904950-72-8 (pb)

BLAIR

He is therefore the last prime minister of the 20th century and one of the most controversial ones, being frequently accused of abandoning cabinet government and introducing a presidential style of leadership.

by Mick Temple
is a senior lecturer in Politics and Journalism at Staffordshire University.
ISBN 1-904950-73-6 (pb)

THE 20 BRITISH PRIME MINISTERS OF THE 20TH CENTURY

www.hauspublishing.co.uk

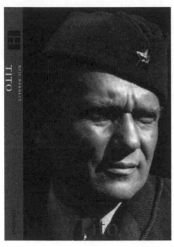

TITO
by Neil Barnett
ISBN 1-904950-31-0 (pb)

Tall, strikingly handsome, powerfully charismatic, the young Croatian motor engineer called Josip Broz was the kind of man you noticed – but only when he wanted you to notice him.

'He had the knack', writes Neil Barnett, biographer of the man who would become Tito, 'of fading into the background to avoid trouble, yet at the same time coming to the fore to demonstrate his abilities.'

These were qualities that served him well as a secret revolutionary Communist, underground and on the run for much of the 1930s, and served him again when outnumbered and outgunned, his Partisans fought the Germans and their Balkan allies through the Second World War.

Barnett traces Tito's long personal road from Moscow Communist to patriotic revolutionary. It was an identity shift that many others would have liked to achieve: that Tito alone defied Stalin to his face and survived built a unique mystique. It was a mystique that was powerful enough to invent the country called Yugoslavia.

Tito used that authority to build the unitary Yugoslavia out of disparate and competing territories and ethnic groups, employing a mixture of persuasion and vicious repression. His achievement was that his Yugoslavia remained stable for so long. The tragedy was that when Tito ended – overweight, and grotesquely festooned with medals and distinctions he had awarded himself – Yugoslavia ended too. It was a country that could only be contained by his personal prestige, writes Barnett: perhaps uniquely in 20th century Europe, Tito's personality is the most important clue to his country's history.